THE
SECRET
LANGUAGE
OF FILM

JEAN-CLAUDE CARRIÈRE

THE
SECRET
LANGUAGE
OF FILM

Translated from the
French by Jeremy Leggatt

faber and faber
LONDON · BOSTON

First published in the USA in 1994
by Random House, Inc.

First published in Great Britain in 1995
by Faber and Faber Ltd
3 Queen Square London WC1N 3AU

Printed in England by Clays Ltd, St Ives plc

© Jean-Claude Carrière

Translation © Jeremy Leggatt

A CIP record for this book is available from
the British Library

ISBN 0-571-17429-9

10 9 8 7 6 5 4 3 2 1

CONTENTS

THE
SECRET
LANGUAGE
OF FILM

INTRODUCTION

I n the years following the First World War, French
colonial administrators in Africa frequently put on
film shows. Their aim was of course to amuse, to enter-
tain in the latest style, but it was also to demonstrate to
subject African populations the unassailable supremacy
of the white nations. The cinema, one recent invention
among many of the industrial West, was the product of
a historic encounter of theatre, vaudeville, music hall,
painting, photography, and a whole series of technical
advances. As such, it helped sing the praises of the white
middle-class civilization that had given it birth.

A sheet was stretched between posts, the mysterious
device was carefully set up, and suddenly, out in the dry
night of the African bush, moving pictures appeared.

African notables and religious leaders invited to
these performances could hardly refuse to attend: such a

breach of manners would surely be interpreted as un-
friendly or even rebellious. So they and their retainers
came. But since these dignitaries were for the most
part Muslim, a long and strict tradition forbade them to
depict the human face and form, God's creation. Did
that ancient prohibition also apply to this new kind of
representation?

Some believers sincerely thought so. They diplomat-
ically accepted official invitations, shook French hands,
and took the seats reserved for them. When the lights
went down and the first beams flickered from the curious
apparatus, they shut their eyes and kept them shut
throughout the performance. They were there and not
there. They were present, but they saw nothing.

I have often wondered what invisible, soundless film
was shown during those few short hours. What went on
behind those African eyelids? Images pursue us even
when our eyes are closed. We can neither escape nor
obliterate them. In the case of the Africans, what was
seen? By whom? And how?

And sometimes I think we ourselves are not very
different from those African Muslims when we go to see
a film. Unlike them, we keep our eyes open in the dark,
or we think we do. But do we not harbor deep within us
some taboo or habit or faculty or obsession that blinds
us to all or to part of the audiovisual band that flickers
fleetingly before us?

How many times could we say, of ourselves or of
others, that a film has not been seen, or truly seen? For
many reasons, some of which are unclear and some we
cannot admit to, we see imperfectly. We refuse to see, or
else we see something else. There is in every film a

4

region of shadow, a stockpile of the not-seen. It can be put there by its authors, knowingly and deliberately. And it can be brought there during a performance by a particular spectator (just one spectator who on that one day is unable or refuses to see everything), or else by that remarkably cohesive group whose reactions are collective even when unpredictable, the entity known as the audience.

Some people believe that in a museum one should move as quickly as possible from one painting to another, never lingering lest a fresh and powerful impression give way to cold analysis. Some pundits even advise us not to read books, merely listen to people speaking about them.

Such paradoxes are difficult to apply to cinema. I can, of course, choose to see only part of a film; I can leave the movie house; or I can stay to see the film a second time. But I cannot see it more or less slowly than the people around me. We are traveling on the same train.

This book, the fruit of a career that almost always favors action over reflection, has no other purpose than to help us—if we so desire—to open our eyes a little wider.

A FEW WORDS
ABOUT A LANGUAGE

In those same African lands, in the early days of cinema, when less intransigent spectators did open their eyes to the novel spectacle, they understood it only with difficulty. Even when they recognized a few of these images from elsewhere—a car, a man, a woman, a horse—they could not connect them. The action, the story, eluded them. Raised in a rich and vital oral tradition, they could not adapt to this succession of silent images, the absolute opposite of what they were used to. They were baffled. A man had to be stationed by the screen for the duration of the film to explain the action. Luis Buñuel even encountered this custom (which survived in Africa into the 1950s) during his childhood in Spain, around 1908 or 1910. A standing man armed with a long pointer picked out the characters on the screen and explained what they were doing. He was called the *explicador.* He vanished—from Spain at least—around 1920.

I imagine that examples of this kind crop up more or less everywhere. For the cinema had brought with it a new—an utterly new—language, which few spectators could absorb without effort, without help.

This was not the case at the very beginning (or so at least we assume). In the first ten years, a film was still just a sequence of static shots, the direct offspring of the theatrical vision. Events necessarily followed one another in unbroken sequence within that static framework, and you could follow the action quite easily. The first audience reaction was of another kind: people wondered exactly what this moving image was made of; seeing in it a kind of new reality, they looked for illusion, for the trick. But once past the first gasp, once it was clear that the Lumière Brothers' train was not going to squash spectators flat, audiences quickly grasped the orderly reel-by-reel sequence of events, fictitious or imaginary, unfolding before a stationary camera. After all, it was not unlike what went on in the theatre, where the stage was static and clearly demarcated. Characters entered that frame, met each other, and exchanged gestures, or rather signals. When they left the camera's field, it was as if they were exiting to the wings. And since they lacked speech and (almost always) color, lofty minds concluded that the whole thing was decidedly inferior to real theatre.

An authentically new language did not emerge until filmmakers started to break the film up into successive scenes, until the birth of montage, of editing. It was here, in the invisible relationship of one scene to the next, that cinema truly sired a new language. In the heat of its own implementation, this seemingly simple technique generated a vocabulary and grammar of unbelievable diversity. No other medium boasts such a process.

We can attempt to describe it first in elementary terms. A man, in a closed room, approaches a window and looks out. Another image, another "shot," succeeds the first. We are shown the street, where we see two characters—the man's wife, for instance, and her lover.

For us today the very juxtaposition of those two images, in that order, and even in the inverse order (beginning in the street), clearly tells us, without our needing to think about it, that the man, through the window, *sees* the wife and lover in the street. We know; we see him in the act of seeing. We effortlessly and correctly interpret those juxtaposed images, that language. We no longer even notice this elementary, automatic, reflexive linkage; like a kind of extra sense, this aptitude is now part of our perceptual system. Eighty years ago, however, it constituted a discreet but real revolution; hence the essential role of the *explicador*, following the characters with his pointer and saying, "The man looks through the window . . . He sees his wife with another man in the street . . ." And perhaps, if the next picture for example showed the watching husband's enraged face, close to the camera this time (a new act of daring, new change of angle, new size of picture, new use of space), the *explicador* would go on: "The man is furious. He has just recognized his wife's lover. He thinks murderous thoughts . . ."

From the first sequences of drawings by prehistoric artists right down to the magic lantern's succession of slides, the human hand and eye have toiled tirelessly and sometimes with astonishing success to show us the impossible—to show us movement in a static image. From that standpoint alone, the cinema represented a prodigious technical leap.

But the true innovation—sweeping, never before seen and perhaps never dreamed of—lay in the juxtaposition of two animated scenes, *one of which canceled out its predecessor by following it.*

Let us stay for a moment with the man who spies his nemesis through the window. Now the wife takes leave of her lover and turns toward home. She looks up, sees her husband at the window, and freezes. We can almost feel her heart pounding.

If at this moment the husband is filmed from the wife's point of view, from directly below, he will inevitably look threatening, overwhelming. The camera position alone will produce this effect, irrespective of our own feelings. And on the other hand, if we see the wife from the husband's standpoint, from above, she will look fearful, vulnerable, guilty.

Let us imagine that the scene takes place at night. If the director decides to place his lights so that the husband's face is lit from below, making teeth glitter, exaggerating cheekbones and browridges (a staple of horror movies), the man will look cruel and terrifying. Soft, impressionistic lighting can, on the other hand, make him look forgiving. Comedy has always called for bright, cheerful lighting: frivolity shuns gloom. Entertainment shies from harsh contrasts—or it used to, for here too fashions are changing fast. It is all part of the living and maturing of a language.

To return for a moment to our trio. This example, as simple as it is possible to get, can instantly turn complicated, for the cinema, armed with new weapons of obvious potential, had soon thrust its way into the world of the mind, into the imaginings, memories, and dreams of its characters. Especially silent cinema, which possessed neither dialogue nor soliloquy to inform us about feelings (the husband's anger, for example) or about more secret thoughts, about everything we call "state of mind." Thus, in the space of a few short years, empirically, with both failures and successes, the most astonishing of grammars was elaborated.

A fairly primitive code soon emerged. If, after the shot of his irate face, we see the man savagely strangling his wife, we can assume that this is real, that we are witnessing the predictable outcome in the conjugal bedroom a few hours later. But if, after that bedroom scene, we return to the irate face, to the husband still looking through the same window and seeing the same characters on the street, a kind of secret instinct tells us that the strangling scene did not really happen, that it was inserted simply to show us the wronged husband's fantasy, his secret wish, perhaps even his firm intention, but one which he has not yet carried out.

If the authors of the film want us to know immediately that this takes place in the mind, they could even make use of a mechanical device, make the picture wobble or gently dissolve or cloud over. This outward change, however naive or elementary it may seem today, was enough to tell certain audiences that a brief flight from reality was taking place.

Let us imagine another device. The man looks into

the street, we see what he sees, then wife and lover fade suddenly into the air and vanish. Now we see the empty street. We return to the man's face, and down that face a tear trickles.

Here we had not witnessed a real scene, but an illusion. The unhappy husband (or possibly widower) was looking at a scene that had taken place on that same spot a little bit earlier.

And so on: he could have seen himself beside the woman; could have seen a skull beneath the lover's hat when the latter turned to face the window; or suddenly have seen a woman other than his wife, wearing the same clothes. In each case the sequence taken as a whole would have told a different story, and the new language would have adapted to fit it.

Thus cinema creates a new space with a simple shift of viewpoint. For example, a man's eyes roam over a crowd, then stop. If at this point we move immediately to another character, we know the first man is looking at him. Something—if the directions of the gaze are well established—demonstrates that relationship beyond a doubt.

The second character is detached, isolated; whether he realizes it or not, he is put into a direct relationship with the first man. An illusory relationship (for they are not in the same picture), but a strong and unmistakable one.

Nothing in the history of artistic expression had suggested that such a relationship-by-juxtaposition might ever be possible.

These narrative procedures, these pairings, these impressions, the new forms given to feelings by these astonishing linkages and dislocations of image, were received in the early 1920s with amazement and passionate enthusiasm, attested a thousand times over. In 1923, still a student in Madrid along with Federico García Lorca and Salvador Dali, Luis Buñuel sent to Paris for reels illustrating these and other techniques, such as accelerated-motion filming, image by image, that allowed you to *see what had never been seen,* for example the germination and growth of a plant. Full of enthusiasm, he organized lectures in Madrid and personally introduced these wonders. A little later, in 1926, Jean Epstein wrote: "The grammar of film is peculiar to film."

Everyone was amazed. After a quarter-century as peepshow entertainment, generally denigrated by the arbiters of taste, the cinema was finally hailed as the latest art form, a form sure to eclipse all others. An American critic, who saw the camera as a machine for turning time into space and vice versa, was soberly calling cinema "the greatest philosophical surprise since Kant."

Here, beyond a doubt, was a truly new language, so much so that the particular effects it used soon became conventional international signs, a sort of planetary code. You manipulated the image differently according to whether you wanted to suggest a dream (in which case the subject's eyes first closed), recollection, or the urge to act. The performer's face, particularly his eyes, projected and received signs which organized the narrative and established feelings. The images spoke around his gaze.

And they spoke for everyone. Unlike writing, in which words always conform to a code you have to know or decipher (you *learn* to read and write), the moving

13

image was within everyone's reach. A language not only new but universal: an ancient dream.

Little by little, as cinema aged—and it aged at top speed, swept along by the momentum of this swiftest-moving of centuries—these writerly procedures that made up the new language tended to take a back seat, almost to disappear. As if, having quickly become a familiar part of our personal baggage, they were no longer deemed necessary. A language scarcely born was already dying. In *Belle de Jour* in 1966, Luis Buñuel abruptly interrupted a scene of Catherine Deneuve climbing a staircase in an unknown house to show a scene in which a little girl appears. He did it without any noticeable change in the image, without any kind of signal (wobble, blur, dissolve, switch from color to black and white) to tell us—as would have been the case thirty years earlier —that we were leaving the story's mainstream. And yet we know at once ("we" meaning here in Europe and in the United States, but possibly not elsewhere), and with virtually no possibility of error, that this little girl is Séverine herself, the character played by Catherine Deneuve, but Séverine as a little girl. With the suddenness and impertinence that can mark our most personal feelings, these visual memories have assailed her as she goes up this very ordinary staircase.

In the case of *Belle de Jour* we are helped by a voice, the mother's. As the memory-frame opens she calls the little girl by her name: "Séverine!" Since we already know the character's first name, this cry (unavailable to the makers of silent film, who would have had to seek a different and possibly more creative solution), this cry orients us painlessly. Today it looks almost too pat. Almost thirty years later, in 1993, this 1960s-style signpost would probably in its turn seem unnecessary and would be dropped. And Buñuel might perhaps move from one image to the other without any precaution of this kind, as he has done in *The Discreet Charm of the Bourgeoisie,* as others do.

The astonishing thing is that as our century progresses we are still somehow managing to keep up with this bizarre linguistic evolution. What is at work here is a circular, hidden relationship between those who make and those who view films, an area no one ever sees but which is the province of many eyes. The makers of films, who are themselves viewers of films made by others, have a rough idea of whether or not they will be understood by their contemporaries. The latter, for their part, adapt (unwittingly, often unconsciously) to forms of expression which briefly seem daring but quickly become commonplace. The first man to make the image waver in order to signal a shift in perception was a genius of a kind. The second copied the first, perhaps improving on the process. By the third time the trick was already a cliché.

In a visual medium nothing is more immediately perceived by an audience than an old familiar trick, something already seen, something already done. Audiences either reject it or welcome it as an old friend. The familiar is comfortable and reassuring. Others have used it (a director might say), so why shouldn't I? But it can also bore an audience, impair its concentration. A calculated risk. Clearly we cannot invent a whole new written language for every book. But a language in a state of permanent self-discovery, a language permanently shaping and enriching itself, obviously cannot just rehash the same old ingredients. It would soon degenerate into empty words. It must innovate, dare—and occasionally fail—to tell and to show.

Almost at the outset of the adventure, filmmakers realized that memory for images can sometimes be stronger and more enduring than for words and sentences. We remember a woman's white body, or a fire aboard a red ocean liner, more accurately and probably more vividly than words that more or less well describe that body or that blazing ship. We are in any case dealing with a different order of memory, another memory altogether, which different peoples can share no matter what language they speak.

All expression—pictorial, theatrical, or merely social —lives on acknowledged or unacknowledged memories, personal reminiscences, a private or communal treasury that glitters brightly for some and less so for others. And everyone finds his voice, his stance, or his coloration in these deep woods we all inhabit—a stance and coloration which others will one day rediscover and remember.

The cinema made lavish use of all that had gone before. When it was given speech in 1930 it called on the services of writers; when color came along it enlisted painters; it turned to musicians and architects. Each contributed his own vision, his own voice.

But it fashioned itself first and foremost from itself. It invented itself and at once copied itself, reinvented itself, and so forth. It even invented hitherto unknown trades: cameraman, director, editor, sound engineer, who all gradually sharpened and perfected their tools.

And it was through the repetition of forms, through daily contact with all kinds of audiences, that the language took shape and branched out, with each great filmmaker in his own way enriching the vast invisible dictionary we all now consult. A language that goes on changing week by week and day by day, the swift-moving reflection of those obscure, many-faceted, complex and contradictory relationships that are the unique connective tissue of human societies.

And how very swift-moving!

In less than half a century, the cinema has lived through everything that happened between Racine's soliloquies and Surrealist poetry, between Giotto's frescoes and Kandinsky's paintings. It is an art on the move, a hurried art, a ceaselessly jostled and dislocated art, and this sometimes leads filmmakers to see profound change in mere syntactical shifts, in new equipment, satellite broadcasting, electronic imaging. This wealth of invention, which film has known since its beginnings, this apparently unlimited extension of the language's instruments (although not of the language itself, which, as we shall see, keeps on running up against the same barriers), often engenders a kind of intoxication which once again leads us to mistake technique for thought, technique for emotion, technique for knowledge. We mistake the *outward signs* of change for the underlying essence of film, and the astounding proliferation of images following us wherever we go only heightens the intoxication and further blurs the essential. How often have we heard (and said): there is nothing film cannot do or show! Other art forms seem to lag far behind, out of breath, exhausted. Constantly dazzled by technical progress, we filmmakers tend to forget substance and meaning—which are true and rare—and see only the same routines repeated in the latest technological disguise. We believe we are looking, but we delude ourselves. Without knowing it, we are like those African dignitaries: having too much to see, our eyes often no longer see at all.

Hence this confusion we see all around us, this sense of constant "revolution," of fever and dissatisfaction, of an almost pathological compulsion to change outward forms—and to mistake the process for true change.

There is no young answer to the old question. The evolution of cinematographic language, particularly of montage, has been swift and far-reaching. So much so that in pretelevision days newly released prison inmates, starved of films for ten years or so, often had trouble grasping what happened on cinema screens. The new films moved too fast for them.

With the video—a barely comprehensible genre in which shapes are too fleetingly perceived for us to appreciate or even identify them—that evolution has entered an entirely new phase. Accelerated montage effects are scarcely new (they have been around since 1920), but for a long time they were merely aesthetic experiments, akin to abstract painting or to atonal music. Hand in glove with the more extreme forms of pop music, however, these same montage effects have moved center stage. The sound volume of these clips remains fairly constant (in other words extremely high) no matter how far we are from musicians and singers, but the images follow one another in a series of unexpected jolts, in spasmodic shifts of shape and angle. It is as if they sought to fragment and scatter our powers of perception, with the apparent intention of eliminating awareness and perhaps even vision.

It is a language both dislocated and effusive. It makes no demands on the mind, for it seeks to deny brain and eye the time they need to establish contact, just as it seeks to short-circuit the optic nerve, stimulating vision and hearing directly, without benefit of a middleman. As if to say: this is as far as I go; this is where I stop; you no longer perceive me, you merely see and hear me.

Seeing without looking, hearing without listening. In the manic frenzy of some videos, there is the sinister vision of a prison in which crazed inmates thrash about. There they are, penned inside that flat, projected image by the borders of the TV or cinema screen. Searchlights glare from the watchtowers, and the captive singers seem to howl their physical despair at being only images in a cage.

I have just spoken of the brain, which misses nothing, even though it can sometimes be dulled and lulled. Those who have studied the brain (Gerald Edelman calls it "the most complex object in the universe") say that the center of language is located on the left, where reason, logic, memory, and the intelligent linking of ideas and perceptions occur. Visual capacity, on the other hand, lives on the right, along with imagination, intuition, and music.

Proper brain function supposes that the two hemispheres work in harmony through countless small, swift linkages. If that is true, then no brain functions on a broader front or with more intensity than that of a great filmmaker, constantly required to fuse the verbal and the visual.

However, the Japanese are said to have their language center on the right, together with images and music. Everything on the same side—which does not stop them making films every bit as good as ours!

I have just written a quite brief passage about the brain, using a conventional typographical device to separate it from what precedes and what follows it. When such a device appears in midchapter it suggests—but does not mandate—a break. I appear to have reached the end of one phase of my writing and to be ready to begin another. The reader may close the book and take a breather before going on—always supposing he wants to go on.

I can think of no cinematic equivalent for this kind of pause, for this identifying peculiarity of written language. Its duration is at the reader's discretion; I use it in my own books because I like coming across it in other people's books. First of all, while viewing a film I cannot stop along the way (unless I have it on a cassette). I accept the requirement of viewer passivity: I let myself go, and like the rest of the audience I am swept along. If the director inserts a physical break in a film—a series of black-and-white images, for example (or a commercial)— he commits an arbitrary act whose high-handedness may jolt and irritate me, an act I might well reject. In a book, the eye can disregard the suggested break and leap forward at once to the continuation of the text. In a film, the break becomes mandatory, and space is transformed into time. And that time threatens to disrupt the narrative, to undermine its interest, even though the filmmaker may consider this moment's respite essential, a sort of wayside halt within the story to view a sunset or a sublime landscape.

But it has its risks. Ever higher risks. Screenplays dropped off at French television studios are often disfigured by script editors with the red-pencil margin warning *danger de zapping*, roughly translatable as "beware channel-hopping." Meaning, cut to the chase! step up the pace! don't dilly-dally! the other networks are breathing down our necks, let's not waste time and lose viewers with all this soporific beauty!

And if I am at home one evening watching a film on TV (for that is where we usually see films, or see them for the second time) and I lose patience with the kind of lull I have gradually grown unaccustomed to, or am annoyed by the intrusion of an unwanted commercial, I quickly switch to another channel with the remote control. And if I find an arresting picture there, I forget all about the first film; the new one has my whole attention. But of course I am just as likely to drop this channel in favor of a third, and so on. Thus—an accidental author abetted by chance—I recreate singlehanded the welter of pictures and sounds that now make up the fabric of so many of our evenings. Channel-hopping has become an objective form of creation. Like it or not, the small black remote-control device is the latest personal filmmaking tool.

By the same token, this individual achievement, which in certain cases might already be called self-expression, and which may one day be designated art, this "personal statement" made by pressing the remote-control switch, almost always unconsciously, is state-of-the-art cinematographic creation; the very latest avatar of a language unknown to us a hundred years ago.

In the early days, cinema wrote before it knew how to write, before it even knew it was writing. The language's Eden.

As in a well-constructed screenplay, action preceded intention. Only one thing counted: solving technical problems in order to tell a story clearly. Filmmaking launched boldly into the adventure. Just like a man forced to make his own way in life, or like a man marooned in a wild land of unknown customs and language, and who gradually discovers ways of making himself understood, of involving others, of getting by with their help.

In the beginning, obviously, the whole point was to show everything. No shadow zones in the picture. Broad static shots, simple movements, unambiguous emotions. The triumph of the seen. Actors exaggerated every move, rolled their eyes, wrung their hands. They were urged to make situation and action crystal-clear, and in any case they were the heirs of a theatrical tradition that favored declamation and posturing, that for example barred women—simply as a matter of elegance and propriety —from dropping their hands below the waist. So now, frustrated of the chance to declaim, they compensated to the best of their ability. Posture was also a means of expression; movement was a sign. They wore exaggerated makeup. Four or five basic feelings were enough.

And directors turned films out at top speed; there was no time to polish. That would come later, when the cinema discovered mystery and equivocation, when it discovered all the things that no longer needed to be shown. But back then, with the help of painted backdrops, Bengal lights, odds and ends of costumes, and throngs of extras, seven or eight scenes sufficed to reconstruct the Trojan War and the last days of Pompeii.

The cinema has always had this urge to jump in with both feet, this eager acceptance of the unplanned, of the impulsive, of the vulgar. It goes back to the origins, to the first unfettered twenty years before fashion (once the so-called Great War was out of the way) got its hooks into the "seventh art." Before the intellectuals (starting around 1925) launched into long, subtle analytical treatises which by now would fill several gigantic and occasionally fogbound freighters. You could, and still can, become a great and respected artist through film, without the help of university degrees or a private fortune. But it's getting harder.

Nor is there any reason to deplore the procession of critics tramping its way through a century extraordinarily given to commentary and to gloss (even more so than the sixteenth century, long held to have dominated the field), or to regret the endless parade of books and lectures, of seminars and colloquia. Obviously the cinema could not remain a carnival attraction, forever parroting the same vocabulary. Every inch of the short but well-traveled road from Chaplin's slapstick antics at Keystone to the magnificent moments of *The Great Dictator* or *Monsieur Verdoux* had to be covered. It was done with understandable pride, for what other century could boast of inventing a new art form? Of placing a new mirror before humankind? It was indeed something to wonder at, to take pride in, to reflect on, particularly since all the way along that short road the language of cinema has constantly expanded, shifted, adapted to changing tastes. An essential evolution, for forms that merely repeat themselves quickly die of sclerosis.

So many experiences in just one century! In the history of cinema two things stand out for me: haste and accumulation. All this jostling, this dashing in every direction, this eternally frustrated battle to organize the flow of things, to stabilize production, to install a new cult complete with gods and high priests, all these breakthroughs in the most unexpected countries, these group journeyings, these solo explorations—no doubt it all had to happen. There is even a breed of aficionados perverse enough to scan film track for that rare black frame overlooked by projectionists or assistant editors. And having isolated that one frame—the briefest of nights sandwiched between sunlit images—no doubt they hurry home to gloat over their find.

No, we should regret none of it. Even though all this haste and fury have gradually spawned the (sometimes desperate) realization that cinema's stream flows faster than others, that its tastes gobble one another up, that the river we ride flows through rapids and over falls, that classics are quickly forgotten, that innovations soon age, that inspiration can abruptly desert us.

At the beginning of this century people wrote just the way they write today. Jarry, Kafka, Chekhov, Proust, Schnitzler, and so many others are our contemporaries. Their work affects us directly, with no need for modification. As for painting, it is obvious that every form in existence today had been discovered and was on public display by 1914.

But in the course of this same century, the young language of film has undergone unbelievable diversification, and it continues to seek and explore. The emergence of new images and new projection techniques, the stubborn war waged against the flat, the enclosed, the framed—the imprisoning tyranny of a rectangle flattened against a wall—everything, including commercial disappointments, helps to sharpen and develop this language. Occasionally, as if defeated by the hardships of the endless quest, some of us are tempted to stop, to say that's it, we're there, our vocabulary is complete, our syntax has been perfected. About the relative size of frames, about light densities and camera movement, we know everything. Nothing much remains to be discovered, we proclaim. Let us now codify once and for all what we know.

This is a recurring temptation with all makers of forms. As the 1940s drew to a close, teachers in the early film schools (who were themselves filmmakers) actually measured film. "A reverse shot of a face that listens but doesn't speak should never exceed forty-eight frames," they would tell their students. Others, in production offices, laid down commercial axioms for posterity: "The hero has to die at the end," or "No film about the Middle Ages," or "Avoid the boxing world like the plague," or else "Never the word 'death' in a title." Many agreed that a film should under no circumstances last longer than ninety minutes.

Faced with such hard-and-fast rules, filmmakers

began to wonder whether the language of cinema, by now indistinguishable from one film to the next, was still alive. A living language, as linguists stress, is one in which you still make mistakes. A perfect language is dead. It neither changes nor hesitates. It has the rigidity of corpses, which make no mistakes.

Luckily these were gossamer rules, instantly blown away. No manual of film grammar—aesthetic, practical, commercial—survives longer than ten years. Everything constantly takes itself apart and reassembles itself. And to complicate things, certain changes seem to run away from the very people who put them into practice. For example, the closeup of a human gaze. In the early days, when an actor looked at another actor off-camera, he looked distinctly away from the lens. He fixed his eyes two or three feet to the right or left as required, generally staring at a board held up by an assistant or at some impassive stand-in.

Little by little, more or less everywhere, that look crept closer to the camera. The angle closed. In the 1960s the actor looked at a face stuck against the camera. In the 1970s he looked at the very edge of the apparatus. Today he looks at a piece of tape stuck beside the lens. Tomorrow he will perhaps look straight into the camera.

Why this progressive change? I am not sure. Possibly to enhance the sense of contact, to compete with the eye-to-eye intimacy of TV announcers. Or perhaps for other reasons which would repay intelligent study.

Permanent flux. No such thing, at the moment, as a clear and reliable cinematic grammar.

* * *

It would therefore be pointless, and probably boring, for me to launch into even a brief description of this language of images, glances, sounds, movements, cries, moments of respite, charm, suffering, slow and accelerated motion, play, braggadocio, effort, loves, secrets—of everything that (at the best of times) constitutes our daily activity. The list is long, indeed endless. It is by now part and parcel of our way of thinking and feeling, the more so since technology fosters arithmetical diversification of this language: we know that two different actors will play the same scene quite differently, and that two editors, using the same filmed material but ordering it differently, can trigger diverse and even contradictory emotions, or give the story a whole new meaning. They say that by selecting a mediocre actor's finest moments, a good editor can make him a credible candidate for acting awards.

Not only is the language complex, since it addresses itself to each individual spectator as well as to the audience as a whole (whose reactions can change from one performance to the next), but everyone speaks it in his own way, with his own tools and ideas, if possible in his own style, with his own limitations and idiosyncrasies.

Peter Brook often says that directing a play is an attempt to make the invisible visible. The image of the final encounter with an audience exists from the moment work begins, in the very choice of the play. But it exists like an uncertain shape in a fog. All the work to come must focus on clarifying that shape, making it living and palpable. Along the way, inevitably, the fog will lift and precise outlines slowly emerge. We will see what we could not see—the way an image slowly swims into focus in a viewfinder.

Making the invisible visible: could that be the proper use for all language? Cinema has never traveled alone. No one, no matter how intent on solitude, no matter how convinced that he is alone, ever journeys without a companion. Intentionally or not, the cinema has coexisted, sometimes most eagerly, with every other medium. Now, in the last fifty years, the theatre has laid great stress on the *unspoken,* on the *subtext.* We have looked more for what happens between Chekhov's lines than for what the lines themselves say (luckily a lot happens between Chekhov's lines). And just as nonfigurative art leaves lots of room (and even at times all the room) to the beholder's imagination, so music, seeking vibrations lost between the notes, beyond the melody, has discovered other, less frequented regions. In a celebrated remark, Sacha Guitry once said, "The concerto you have just heard was by Wolfgang Amadeus Mozart. And the silence that followed was also by Mozart." A certain number of contemporary musicians say their principal goal is to move from one silence to the next silence. Just as for Jerzy Grotowsky the art of dance is most clearly manifest when the dancers' feet are not touching the ground, we too have all dreamed upon the ephemeral, the featherlight, the airborne, all the things you say without saying and show without showing. Most often blindly, we have stretched invisible threads between signs we found too visible, too striking, too weighty.

All this is situated inside the secret workings of time, inside the dim recesses of our century, inside those accumulated forces too somber and too dense ever to be analyzed in the bright light of day. Science itself, at its cutting edge, focuses more on relations among facts, and on the almost unfathomable forces that determine them, than on the facts themselves.

Our whole century, obdurately concrete though it is, seems secretly obsessed with creating multiple embodiments of the unseen. The cinema, naturally, has partaken of that search. Sometimes it has even led the way. As its role required, it has shown us moving images, but it has also shown us unsuspected affinities among those images. By tacking two shots together it confronted characters who in reality follow one another, thus upsetting the normal hierarchy of objects in space (D. W. Griffith is credited with this find). It has shown monstrously enlarged human faces and even, in *Un Chien Andalou (An Andalusian Dog)*, a closeup of a razor slicing through an eyeball (women in the audience fainted). It has invented accents, raptures, griefs, new kinds of terror. It may even have helped us discover hitherto unknown feelings in ourselves.

Thus, through the ceaseless technical fever that is its hallmark, the cinema (even though it can seem hurried, at times even convulsive, excessive, earsplitting) has played an irreplaceable role in the exploration of connections. First because it lives exclusively on connections: among images, feelings, characters. But also because its particular technique and language have empowered it to undertake extraordinary voyages of exploration which, without our knowing it, have spilled over into all neighboring forms, perhaps even into our personal conduct.

In the absence of microphones or loudspeakers, nineteenth-century theatre was condemned to declamation. Talking films brought us the murmur, the intimacy of truly confidential exchanges, even the gasp, the heartbeat. They exploited the human gaze with infinite delicacy, and mastered the arts of silence. And from the strange sentiments that animate the human race, they extracted shades of meaning that traditional theatre could never express and that literary fiction approached differently, through the felt (or unfelt) echo of certain words and certain phrases.

The cinema loves silence—and within that silence the sound of a breath being drawn. It is expert at populating silence, at listening to it—sometimes the better to destroy it. It can also pit two silences against one another, as it did in *Les Enfants du Paradis (The Children of Paradise)*, when literally indescribable emotions are seen to flit soundlessly across a mime's chalk-white face.

It is always a beautiful moment on a set when the sound engineer calls for a few minutes of silence. He will record this silence; he needs it. It will be used for something (nobody knows quite what). This real silence does not exist in nature. Even forest depths are alive with rustling sounds. Silence is obtainable only in a well-sealed studio. You turn the red light on and shut all the doors; everything comes to a halt, actors and technicians freeze, stop breathing. You *create* silence.

Earphones clamped to his head, the sound engineer listens to this silence, savors it gravely. You can compare two silences, the way painters can compare two blacks or two whites. No two silences are the same.

Two or three minutes go by. No one stirs. Your mind is a blank. And then it is over: the sound engineer is satisfied. He thanks everyone, sounds slowly resurface, and you move on to the next scene.

Born silent, the cinema continues to love silence. But it can also love the ambiguity and amorphousness of feeling. In this respect it has known unbelievable change over the past sixty years, from its wildly gesticulating beginnings to the present inscrutability of certain screen faces. Nowadays, simply from the demeanor or expression of particular actors, we pick up a clear message, depending on our mood of the moment, on the day, on the theatre we happen to be in, or on the spectators around us. (For the African dignitaries with their closed eyes, these immediate reactions were indeed the only possible guide.) But we also glean nothing specific, nothing identifiable, nothing definable. A new bend in the road can be suddenly revealed by a glance or a shrug, a bend of which we can say nothing, for it is something we have no words for, and yet we sense that it contains something meaningful.

Occasionally, this language has ventured in directions never before explored, to the limits of the possible. In *Persona*, which he made in 1966, Ingmar Bergman shows us an actress, Liv Ullmann, who abruptly ceases to speak. She is in the care of a nurse, Bibi Andersson, who unlike her babbles endlessly. In a long scene around the middle of the film, the nurse tells her patient an erotic story that takes place on a beach, a story she says she had a part in. That story lasts eight minutes; not for a second do we leave the face, in closeup, of the nurse telling it. Then we move to Liv Ullmann's face, and the next eight minutes are taken up by exactly the same story, word for word, and told by the same voice.

Luis Buñuel, himself fascinated by the repetition of an action or a phrase (as can be seen in *The Exterminating Angel,* filmed in 1961), often spoke to me of that apparently bold and unique scene from *Persona.* I had the opportunity of spending time with Bergman in 1972 and I asked him—in Buñuel's name and mine—the inevitable question (which he had doubtless heard a hundred times): "Why that repetition?"

He replied very simply that he had never intended it, either while writing the screenplay or during shooting. He had meant to edit this narrative scene the way such scenes often are edited, cutting several times from one woman's face to the other. Then in the somber calm of the cutting room, he realized that he did not know where to cut, that all that back-and-forth movement introduced strain, disorder, and emotional leaps. Something was not working. He therefore decided to keep both accounts, identical as to wording, visually different, one following the other.

He added, "The story you tell isn't the same as the story you hear."

Bergman also told a press conference one day how the idea for the film *Cries and Whispers* came to him. Several times, as he was thinking of something else, an image appeared to him out of the blue. At first it was quite vague: four white shapes against a red background. He dismissed it, but the image was persistent. Again he tried to dispel it, but it insisted, and he had to yield. He then saw that those four shapes were four white-clad women in a red-lined room.

On the first, almost obsessive image that had forced itself upon him (for without knowing it, he was looking for a film), he set to work. He gave sharp outlines to those fuzzy shapes, gave them faces and names, established relationships among them—a process recalling the vague fog-shrouded shape Peter Brook mentions. Here it was a matter of accepting something ill-defined and leading it toward definition, preserving along the way (as Bergman does in his film) the equivocal moments, the secret passages: for if given free rein, the distinct often tends to become too clear-cut, too dry and cold and uncompromising.

To a call of this kind, to a signal which is at first obviously wordless, almost the fleeting beckoning of a ghost, the cinema must supply a form and of course a language, as personal a language as possible. At the same time it must remain aware that at every moment we depend on everything that surrounds and holds us together. Our personal imagination stems from another imagination, vaster and more ancient than ourselves. We are but one knot in a rug. When the camera moves laterally in an interior in films by the Japanese masters, Kenji Mizoguchi, Akiro Kurosawa, it reproduces as if instinctively the direction and pace of a worshipper visiting a shrine.

Obscurer still: we belong to a species in which right-handers outnumber left-handers. (A rare phenomenon, for animals seem to make little distinction between right and left in using their limbs.)

Whence this right-handed bias, which scientists say makes us unique? No one really knows. Some have sought a link in the direction of our handwriting. It is easier for a right-hander to write from left to right because his hand moves away from his body; a left-hander's pen, however, moves toward his body, constraining him and sometimes obliging him to twist his spine, almost to write from top to bottom. A left-hander is fully at ease only in writing Arabic, which seems to be made for him.

This right-handed dominance appears to be written into some secret place within us. A French neurologist, François Lhermitte, tells this story. Very simply, he draws land going down to the sea, with the sea on the right of the drawing. On the water he sets a sketchily drawn ship, with nothing in the drawing to indicate which is the vessel's bow and which its stern.

Then he asks where the ship is going. A clear majority says the ship is leaving, heading out to sea.

If the drawing is turned around, with no additional changes—the sea on the left and land on the right—the same majority will answer that the ship is about to dock, that it is headed for the land. In other words, for the majority of us the ship always moves to the right.

This habit of seeing and inserting motion where it does not exist has probably been a part of us without our knowing it. It doubtless partly explains why a cameraman's or a director's first impulse is to move the camera to the right or ask an actor to walk from left to right, as if that were the easier and more natural path to take. (What is more, the eyepiece is usually on the left of the camera, which makes it more natural to push it to the right.) Moving in the opposite direction is rarer (this also holds for the theatre). It requires an effort, a decision. It goes against our initial impulse.

Another buried form: for three or four centuries we have got into the habit of looking at world maps with the north above and east to the right. This habit writes into us a geography that is quite arbitrary, since top and bottom and right and left obviously do not exist in the cosmos.

Despite itself, the cinema has acquired this habit. If it needs to show a convoy heading west, it moves it from right to left on the screen. Without realizing it, the filmmaker is echoing the mapmaker's conventions. The other way around—putting the west on the right—would disturb our perception even though we could not say why.

Thus, brand-new though it may be, the cinema is by no means alone and free. Traditional forms, stronger than all others, slip into today's techniques. And despite ourselves, other invisible forms which we bear within us determine how we depict and see the world.

It is probably as hard to write a book about the cinema as it would be to make a film about the language of literature. I cannot use pictures with sound on these pages, and film histories illustrated with movie stills have always struck me as hybrid and illegitimate. So I am making do with a handful of scattered examples in order to tell in words what is perhaps the basic distinctive feature, what in today's jargon would be called the *difference,* of this language.

We know that in the theatre, when an actor comes onstage magnificently costumed, every eye in the auditorium is momentarily fixed upon him. The play itself suffers immediate adverse consequences. For a second it is forgotten, cast aside. Contact is lost, and a path has to be traveled all over again. A mirage, a dangerous embellishment, what is known somewhat contemptuously as an "effect," has just marred the story that had held us, that had seemed essential, what we had presumably come to see.

Literary history is full of flamboyant flourishes of this kind. What is "good writing"? Must the writer array himself at all times in fine phrases, the way some people wear fine clothes, just to lend power and significance to his words? Or must he (as Stendhal recommended) express himself with the dispassionate objectivity of the penal code? A few writers, alive to the twin dangers of platitude on the one hand and superfluity on the other, shuttle constantly between the two temptations (like Flaubert fleeing the flamboyance of *Salammbô* for the dry brevity of *Bouvard and Pécuchet*). Such writers never lose their mistrust of the arrogance, pointlessness, and self-indulgence of a distinctive style. But this phenomenon of style, this obsession with "writing well," in other words with *not* writing like everyone else, with setting your own stamp on words—how do we get rid of it? Is it not truly a part of ourselves? How to attain absolute objectivity?

People believed for a time that cinema's "mechanical eye" could more easily dissolve this literary mirage

—that you had only to set up a camera on a street and let it film passersby to produce a sort of cinematic statement, of *cinéma-vérité*. But what about the frame, closing off its own square of street? What about the motionless lens, and time, which relegates to the past all things filmed? What about our beholding eye, our choice of this particular street? Where is the truth? And which truth?

Even in fictional cinema many directors have attempted to efface their style, make it everyday and conventional, so as to let the film act and speak for itself. Wild camera movements, unusual angles, visual fantasy, distorted sound effects—all seem comparable to the actor's ostentatious costume. Jean-Luc Godard used to say that to make a good film you should never use a zoom lens. Together with a few friends, I too drew up a table of surefire indicators of a bad film. For example, "Any film which shows someone hit by machine-gun fire and *dying in slow motion* is a bad film." Use of such a device, with its mindless determination to (as I heard someone put it) "get the greatest possible mileage out of death," struck us, and still strikes me, as vulgar and obscene. Slow motion (or in other cases accelerated motion) seemed to mark a film as belonging to the horrible and hellish category of movies not to be seen.

Among other stigmata were every kind of gelatinous deformation of the image, particularly the artistically out-of-focus shot; the pair of lovers running to meet in slow motion, arms eagerly outstretched; any scene in which a character puts on clown makeup (unbearably hackneyed); any picture of gulls over the sea (particularly at sunset); and all such cliché horrors.

Such inflexibility did not last. In his later films

37

Godard himself, after working several years with video, became a prolific user of all the latest technical procedures. Fortunately, no rule ever endures!

Yet the instant an effect materializes, we run the risk of seeing technique and only technique. When the camera takes over the screen we feel it at once; we realize suddenly that we are in a movie house—not in the heart of the story we have come to see. This violation is particularly obvious and disturbing in period films. A striking cinematic effect in such a film, set for example in the sixteenth century, has an incongruity which breaks the thread and kills our interest.

I remember how carefully Daniel Vigne set up his camera in *The Return of Martin Guerre,* selecting height of viewpoint, keeping movements imperceptible and always linked to the movement of a given character. Maximum discretion, as if he were apologizing for this intrusion of present-day impedimenta among peasants in sixteenth-century dress. Anyone who has ever attempted to reconstruct the past with maximum fidelity has encountered the same problems and adopted the same kinds of solutions.

Unless you make this irruption, this hiatus, the very heart of the film. Unless the lens's intrusion into the Middle Ages is your real theme. Unless the director chooses to cloak a body he knows to be sickly in a fine garment. Unless . . .

Options that are forever open, in the cinema as elsewhere. Every language tends to branch out, to adorn itself, to preen, or else with a kind of reverse coquetry to wallow in street vernacular. Every language tends to expand and conquer, to be satisfied in the final analysis with itself alone, and often to speak for the sake of speaking. In a way, the Surrealists even sought this autonomy, this omnipotence; they both aspired to and practiced writing in an automatic mode. They believed that words, acting in unmediated contact with ourselves and freed from the mind's control, express things we are too paralyzed by our cultural habits to see or feel any more.

The cinema too has undergone the temptation of "automatic filming," of the strolling camera. (For that matter it has flirted with every great artistic temptation since the 1920s, with results generally short-lived.) The techniques that gave it life had clear, built-in limits. They became and still are a constraint. Film cannot escape its destiny: it can never be anything but a sequence of still photographs stitched together by our eye, which introduces motion into this sequence of motionless units. The movies are exactly that—moving pictures. Within a defined and usually selected frame a film has to show something identifiable. And since production methods are long and sequential, the film never escapes the mind's control.

Although Buñuel had been fascinated since his youth by special effects (even around 1970 I recall his genuine wonder on discovering the special-effects possibilities of video during a Saturday night TV broadcast), he systematically rejected overelaborate or overwhelming shots. He liked them in Fellini, but refused them in his own films. He sought a neutral, almost boring image, at the outer limits of banality. Example: for the end of *Nazarin* his Mexican head cameraman, Gabriel Figueroa, prepared a splendid frame for him, with high mountains in the distance, cacti in the foreground, and fleecy clouds in a vast sky. Without even looking in the view-finder, Buñuel brutally swung the camera around to face in the opposite direction, forcing the whole crew to scramble into new positions, and filmed Francisco Rabal moving away across plowed fields that might have been anywhere.

Buñuel did not want mystery to emanate from a well-contrived chiaroscuro; from the timely creaking of a door, from blurring, from slow motion. He thoroughly distrusted every kind of cinematographic effect, rejecting it as facile, arty. He sought what was unseen rather than what was obscure. He was wary of beauty. Yet rather than seeking (for example) a repetitive formalism on the lines of Yasujiro Ozu's fixed frames and low-angle camera, he saw a mysterious hypnotic power in the trembling of the frame's borders, in the almost imperceptible movement of the camera, like the wavering head of a snake seeking prey.

This concern to suppress technique in favor of something more subtle, this deliberate avoidance of effect, this distrust of ever-seductive beauty seems singularly dangerous. In film, virtuosity is highly reassuring, which is why it so often attracts beginners. Rejecting virtuosity implies that you are sure of the power of what you are showing.

In the 1950s we had a conventional, technically flawless cinema which it suited us to call traditional, but which very soon seemed to be repeating itself. The same designers worked with the same head cameramen and the same editors, so that judging only by directorial style it was often impossible to tell one film from another. People even worried that the language of cinema—indistinguishable from film to film—might have given up the ghost.

In those days the director was just one worker among many. Although he was often the one who had chosen the subject of the film, he concerned himself with little beyond directing the actors and supervising the work schedule. Sometimes, for example in the American production system of the 1930s and 1940s (which, being a strictly industrial vision, is still very much alive and kicking), even the screenplay and the editing were out of his hands. The producer, absolute master of the film, took the footage from him at the end of every day for editing elsewhere. Often the director was nothing but a privileged employee, hopping from one production to the next. The better organized wrapped up one film on Saturday evening and began another on Monday morning.

Today, when a conscientious director spends at least two years of his life on each of his films, and sometimes four or five (often enough, he is his own producer), such practices seem out of the question, except for television series. But in the latter case the director is scarcely more than a faceless technician. During the 1986 Venice Festival, the German director Peter Fleischmann asked an audience of two or three hundred film people:

"Who is the director of 'Dallas'?"

No one could tell him.

There have been upheavals in the brief and tumultuous history of the cinema: the French New Wave, at the end of the 1950s, rose in determined revolt against this systematic anonymity, against this surface similarity among films distinguished by nothing except perhaps their actors and the story they told. One of its cherished aims was for directors to stop concealing their personalities behind assembly-line technique. Its advocates really spoke of "language," of the *caméra-stylo,* or camera-as-writing-instrument, of the *author's film*. Film language —common to everyone and peculiar to each individual, like all language—reappeared on the agenda, for the greater good of film. It emerged from the shadows: you began to see it on the screen, you followed its progress, its maturing, its repetitions, its aberrations, sometimes its disasters.

Fairly soon—for nothing stays fresh and, as the Indian proverb says, "God is always concerned with beginnings"—this notion of the *author's film* was perverted, and the language suffered in consequence. From the splendid declaration we all applauded—"a film must bear the mark of its director"—the formula in fairly short order entered its decadent phase and became more or less "an *author's film* is one in which a director talks about himself." Between the two approaches the gap is narrow, the difference barely palpable. Yet it is complete and it is most often unbridgeable. Slide into the self-indulgence of the second definition, and the great door at once swings open to reveal the endless fevered imaginings that swamped us in the 1970s. This was especially the case in France where so many voice-overs—usually monotonous—droned in slow accompaniment to anemic images. Everyone wanted to "express" his fantasies, his memories, even his personal thoughts. Everyone felt theoretically entitled to do so, and was later painfully surprised to see his work enjoy at most two or three days' screening in a small, empty theatre.

Yet again, in just a few years an idea had been lost. It had slipped from the initial rigor of an exacting theory, which great filmmakers instinctively applied, to the banality of daily (and rote) implementation.

The trend today, for a thousand appropriate reasons, is toward a return—itself dangerous—to a screenwriter's cinema. Here content would outweigh form: the film would be made only to illustrate the screenplay, not the screenplay to allow the film to come to life. I will return later to the difficult role of the screenwriter, always caught between conflicting demands. But let us say that since the 1980s the screenwriter has held the place of honor, of too much honor. All over the world conferences are dedicated to the theme (in my view impossibly refractory) of the screenplay. In particular, who knows why, a thousand seminars bloom on the topic of the *adaptation*. Hence the danger: a return to the literary, a weakening of the image in favor of words. Images constantly falling into the pitfall of the tried-and-true, of the run-of-the-mill. The end of striving, of experimenting.

But this is doubtless just a swing of the pendulum, induced by commercial uncertainties. A swing which I hope will shortly be reversed.

We saw something similar happen in the United States when the talkies took over. Suddenly, just because films spoke, the heads of the major companies decided to call on the masters of the written word, in other words on great writers. They summoned Faulkner, Fitzgerald, Steinbeck, and others. They offered them houses, offices, secretaries, and salaries, and put them to work on what was rather naively assumed to be their domain, words. Amid conflicts, blunders, and much ill-feeling, a long-lived misapprehension arose and endures. It some-times produced excellent results (the collaboration of William Faulkner and Howard Hawks, for example), as well as remarkable disasters. Some historians even speak of a simultaneous decline in the language of film, as if profligate and sometimes excessive use of dialogue in-clined directors to laziness and did away with the need for powerful, compact, radiant, and emblematic frames, each one of which—in great silent films from Fritz Lang to Buster Keaton—had a few years earlier seemed to con-tain the whole film.

Moreover these universal images, once readily un-derstood all over the world, were now displaced by a spoken language that led back to the particular, to the parochial, that now had to be dubbed or subtitled in order to be universally understood.

According to one reporter, William Faulkner, hired to write the screenplay for *The Land of the Pharaohs*, which Howard Hawks was to direct, put off the writing as long as possible. Months went by, Alexandre Trauner's set went up, but not a line was written.

One day Faulkner announced that he had started work. The producer arrived, found the writer splitting his sides with laughter, and asked the reason for his mirth. Faulkner showed him the first line of dialogue. The Pharaoh, visiting the building site, had asked his workers:

"How's it going, boys?"

This simple English phrase he had put in the Pha-raoh's mouth kept Faulkner laughing uncontrollably for hours. But later he did finish the screenplay.

And then, like all fashions, the fashion for great writers passed.

Our century has witnessed the invention of a language and daily observes its metamorphosis. Seeing a language come to life, a true language able to say anything, and participating, even if only as a spectator, in that ongoing process of discovery, strikes me as a unique phenomenon that should excite semiologists, psychologists, sociologists, and anthropologists. But perhaps that language has grown too familiar to us—too little noticed, even—to continue to hold our interest. It has taken only four generations of filmgoers for the language to write itself into our cultural memory, into our reflexes, perhaps even into our genes. The sequences of moving pictures that enfold and submerge us are today so numerous and so interlinked that they could be said to constitute what Milan Kundera calls a "semantic river." In it we and our peers swim effortlessly, buoyed by familiar currents. Only at times of ferocious pollution are we seized with the brutal urge to stem a flow in which facility is drowning us, with the need to cut loose, bind a handkerchief over our eyes, see and hear no more. For a language is also something we can decide to stop understanding; something to refuse, to reject.

Fellini once said that television had spawned a new generation of spectators he found arrogant, overbearing, neurotically impatient. The ability to switch channels at all times, which kills a narrative, to keep on moving ahead to something else (the idea that images I am not seeing are being shown *elsewhere* is intolerable), has created fireworks displays that spurt from our own fingertips. The magic remote control gives us the illusion that these images belong to us, that we have total power over them, that without us they would not be. They are simply images chasing after other images, with no hope of gulping them down. This impatience, said Fellini, could never be satisfied or sated, for we cannot fix our eyes on an image without first eliminating the picture we had been looking at, just as we cannot utter two words simultaneously. It is a vain, futile pursuit, giving birth to fatigue and depression. The spectator himself is destroyed by his own fevered role. The sequence of images cannot resist him. It blows to pieces in his hands. And he founders along with it.

Whether you speak it or are at the receiving end, you must obviously remain in control of any language. To be able to love the cinema fully, you must be able to do without images, without cinema. It is a question of independence. Just as the millers of old heard their mill wheels only when they stopped turning, so we can properly observe the images around us only as long as we retain the strength to extinguish them.

REALITY
IN FLIGHT

I n 1974, the Algerian director Ahmed Rachedi was shooting a film in the mountains of Kabylia, in northern Algeria. For one small part he hired an old woman who spoke only Kabyle and knew little about the cinema.

A young Algerian actor played the part of this woman's son. As required by the script, he was killed by a burst of gunfire in one scene and his body was carried away. On the director's instructions, the old woman wept and showed her grief as well as she was able. Her pain seemed very real.

Next morning, for various technical reasons, they had to shoot the same scene again. Ahmed Rachedi quickly explained the situation to the old woman, asking her to do exactly as before. "We're going to kill your son all over again," he told her. "You just cry the way you did yesterday."

But the woman did not understand. For her, the young actor playing her son had died the day before. With her own eyes she had seen red blood spurt from the little plastic packets which you conceal in clothing and which explode on command. She had seen the young man fall and his body carried away. She had not seen him again that night. For her he was—like other victims in the few films she had seen—dead beyond the shadow of a doubt. In cinema, a highly magical and dangerous activity, people really were killed. The actor had to be brought to her, she had to see him and touch him, before she agreed to reenact the scene of her grief.

But she remained deeply disturbed. In another scene, answering a French policeman who exasperatedly asked her, "But don't you understand Arabic?" she was supposed to give some reply or other, still concerning her son. Instead of saying the lines that had been taught her, she answered the other actor with a simple no. The director stopped shooting, explained to her that she had to "act," to say what was asked of her. She refused to budge, and since she really did speak nothing but Kabyle, stubbornly went on answering no to the question "But don't you understand Arabic?"

She added (in Kabyle), "I'm not going to start lying at my age."

The history of the cinema is studded with such stories, an endless source of wonder to the film workers who pass them around. The Kabyle woman considered her line a lie (and from her standpoint she was right) because of the cinema's mysterious and compelling power to convince. It has possessed this power since its beginnings (and to a greater degree than any other medium), ever since the Lumière Brothers' first Parisian spectators recoiled in alarm at the train hurtling silently down on them.

Here, what is invisible is unreality itself. What the audience does not see is the subterfuge. The fiction, the very nature of film, shooting and projection techniques —everything is forgotten, swept away by the physical power of the talking image, that noisy mask slipped over reality's countenance. Women jump, scream, and hide their faces when a snake suddenly crosses the screen —women and some men, too. Vampires terrify, spires induce vertigo, pornographic movies embarrass the prudish. I even knew an asthmatic who choked when actors smoked on-screen. The cinema has exploited this singular power more or less calculatedly since its adventure first began, since Georges Méliès, not content with inflating human heads or reproducing himself many times over on-screen, actually reconstructed current events, such as the coronation of the king of England, in his studio at Montreuil-sous-Bois.

Of course such tongue-in-cheek "staging" of contemporary history, which seems somewhat barefaced to us, descended directly from popular theatrical tradition. But Méliès did more than just fabricate settings. He was already laying false trails, playing with the new ambiguity. With the merest of hints at the brazenness of his deceptions, he led his audiences on, already aware of the almost inexplicable power of persuasion his moving images possessed.

It was and is a power that sometimes escapes us, that

can let us down just when we count on it. It is a shifting, inconsistent kind of power, often stronger, oddly enough, in the excesses of fiction than in the supposedly objective honesty of the documentary—as if "real" reality were harder to convey than the artificial kind. Indeed, certain famous documentaries in the perverse Méliès tradition (such as Luis Buñuel's *Las Hurdes*) are pure fake, wholly reconstructed and staged, as their authors themselves admit. In such cases subterfuge comes to the rescue of faltering (or at least dull or mediocre) reality, giving it the treacherous allure we too readily accept as the "truth." And thus a new chapter opens in the age-old history of the lie.

The tools of persuasion can seem simple: emotion, a physical sense of fear, repulsion, irritation, anger, distress. But in fact the operation is much more complex, indeed probably beyond definition. It engages the most secret mechanisms of our brain, including perhaps the brain's laziness, its natural indolence, its willingness to surrender its virtue to any smooth talker. And it asks questions (which like all real questions are unanswerable) about the relationship of reality to truth. (Always supposing that those two words, their meaning blunted by long usage, can be linked to the tendency to which we all succumb: our disturbing failure to resist the images put before us, our inability to think for ourselves, to react intelligently and skeptically.) Perhaps there are even grounds for fearing, as some claim, that this perverse taste for illusion, this desperate wish to be convinced, may be the mark of fundamental human duplicity.

* * *

In the 1970s, still in Algeria, filmmakers and doctors made an educational documentary about an eye disease widespread in one of the country's central provinces. Traveling crews then went out to show the film and organize discussions in the villages. The disease, a form of trachoma, is caused by a fly, which was shown in closeup several times on the screen.

After the showing the villagers announced that the film did not concern them. They even seemed surprised that they had been asked to view it.

"But almost every one of you has trachoma!" a doctor said to them.

"Yes, but we don't have flies that size here."

In this case it was the very idea of closeups, the technical concept of lens and visual proportion, that was called into question. Cinematographic language was not perceived as a language, as a conventional vocabulary, and the Algerian mountain people simply saw an enormous fly. Their intelligence and common sense rejected the whole thing. No, they knew of no flies of this size. They were in much the same position as ourselves when we look at the sky. If we did not *know* it was the other way about, if we had not been taught it, we would clearly and unarguably *see* that the sun moves around the earth and is markedly smaller.

Likewise with those Algerian villagers. They had not seen the film, they had seen the fly.

In the 1960s, the French ethnologist-director Jean Rouch shot a film about hippopotamus hunting. He did it with the people of a village located near the Niger River. During the shooting he recorded music in the hunters' village. He then moved to Dakar to edit the film, incorporating this music into the soundtrack.

When the film was finished a few months later, he went back to the village to show it to the inhabitants. It was the occasion for a great all-night celebration. The villagers, who asked to be shown the film six times running, proclaimed themselves delighted. They had no trouble recognizing themselves and families and friends on screen, and even expressed grief at sight of those who had since died.

No problem arose to rival that of the fly closeup. The film, as a film, met with perfect acceptance. And yet, as dawn approached, one or two of them added a comment to the warm compliments they paid Jean Rouch: the music was wrong, quite wrong.

Surprised, Rouch said, "But it's your own music! I recorded it right here!"

"Oh yes," the Africans replied. "We recognized it. But if you played it that way when you went hunting, the hippopotamus would take off in a hurry!"

The whole notion of musical accompaniment was challenged. Jean Rouch tells the story with a smile; he sees it as an object lesson. If you want to be real, you have to be real all the way. Every cultural habit can hide an underlying falsehood. How often do we watch a TV broadcast on Lebanon (or any other cursed or war-ravaged place) without noticing that the producer, to "flesh out" or "strengthen" his pictures, has almost surreptitiously slipped in a musical accompaniment, a few bars of Wagner or Erik Satie or the Talking Heads. Such a procedure is out-and-out falsification: if we were hip-popotamuses we would flee indeed! But most of us do not even notice. We are used to it.

All kinds of alien music surreptitiously invade images we believe to be real, true to life. In the constant shuttling from ourselves to the "real" and back again, the pitfalls are many and hidden, whether it's the closeup of a fly, a musical accompaniment, or any other kind of technical enhancement. In these particular cases our eyes and ears, conditioned for almost a century, are desensitized and virtually disabled. We believe we are truly seeing and hearing, but parasites invade us, intruders seduce us, and without knowing it we are duped. Our mesmerized intelligence shrinks and is paralyzed, yielding to emotion and even sensation, for we sometimes receive the strong physical impression—as in the case of the snake that makes the women swoon—that film, that fine blank membrane on which images settle and move, can touch us directly, that this reptile will slither under every skirt in the auditorium. Our eyes see what is not there, our ears fail to hear what *is* there; the sun goes on circling the earth; in the end we find our pleasure in illusion.

Antonin Artaud wrote: "Cinema plays first of all on the human skin of things, on the epidermis of reality."

Contact between two skins. Relief through touch. Every filmgoer is in his own way a little Doubting Thomas, believing only what he sees, and seeing what he believes he sees. He is hardly ever able to pursue the image outside the screen, to stretch it out, to distort it.

"If the trick is convincingly performed," there is no escaping it. We consent, often happily, to be fooled.

What is the source of this power, which can so often become hypnotic, even hallucinatory?

Photography, no doubt. That is what we are first tempted to reply. The photographic process. Every film is a succession of photographic reproductions, and a photo (whatever you do with it) is always something that has had an existence, that has at some specific point been real. Indeed, the photo is proof (sometimes most tenacious proof) of that existence. In fact, it can be the only proof—witness the efforts of certain regimes to distort the history of the century by banishing nonpersons from the photographic record. (Which can be dangerous, for the very fact of wanting to eliminate them often enhances the importance of such ghosts.)

Every film in its own way manufactures past time; and as we all know, the past is the only unarguable reality, the one that leaves a trail, that can be told and even taught. Films (in which tinkering is trickier than in still photos) will obviously be useful to the historians and archeologists, perhaps even the paleontologists, who will one day mull over twentieth-century events. For historians, this is already the case. Filmed news overflows with images of our time, from war to daily life, sports to accidents, celebrities' lives to disasters. The images are often cropped, manipulated, subtly disfigured by editing or commentary or music (Beirut with "backing" by Wagner). The images can carry a propaganda message, for example, footage of very young Germans departing to their deaths in 1945, full of warrior zeal. Here reality is wholly misrepresented by staging.

You choose the actors (blond, beautiful), you dress them carefully, you ask them to smile at the right moment, just as they march past the camera, you choose a sunny day to shoot (you even boost the sun with artificial lighting). Everything is calculated to make the lie seem true. The march to massacre is a joyful affair.

We are prone to all these distortions, even in peacetime, even dealing with apparently trivial, dull, ordinary events. The network of images that surrounds us is so dense and at times so intricately woven that it is almost impossible not to give way to a kind of mental indolence, an intellectual somnolence which allows the invasion of lies—just as, in days gone by, drunken or exhausted sentinels in beleaguered cities dozed off and let the enemy in. The "truth" of a photo, or of a newsreel, or of any kind of reporting, is obviously quite relative, for we see only what the camera sees, we hear only what we are told. We do not see what someone has decided we should not see, or what the creators of these images did not see. And above all, we do not see what we do not want to see.

One of the latest fashionable tricks—it started in the United States, but there is every reason to believe it is already practiced elsewhere as well—is manufacturing false news reports, filming fake news. We were unable to film this or that historic scene? No problem: we'll reconstruct it, using actors.

It can be done by inserting new images, interleaving them with real-life ones (a well-known editing trick often used to comic effect), or else by purely and simply reconstructing a news item. In July 1989, for instance, during the Felix Bloch spy case, ABC broadcast—as "irrefutable proof"—a scene in which Bloch hands a Soviet agent a briefcase. It was a fake, entirely stage-managed, filmed in realistic conditions.

American law requires that the word *dramatization* appear on-screen at such a point. But this warning can appear so often and so fleetingly that few viewers take notice. Indeed, it is a kind of screen-infesting virus that must sooner or later be driven away. The "America's Most Wanted" series plays skillfully on this confusion. The added-on scenes are so cleverly shot that a certain number of viewers will inevitably be deceived. One actor appearing in the series was arrested and handed over to the police by a viewer who assumed he was the criminal in person.

Here we are close to nineteenth-century melodrama, when audiences are said to have waited at the stage door to give the villain a thrashing. Close also to Méliès, who was the first to put fiction and real life in the same bag.

Simultaneously, in television programming the world over, reality (or fabricated reality) is making a spectacular comeback in the form of *simulations*. Here the two sides of the looking-glass meet and are blurred. Men and women who have suffered some mishap are asked to recreate the episode in question for the cameras. They thus become actors in their own story, which they present to us with all the paraphernalia of fakery and stagesetting. Stray characters drifting in from real life thus get caught in the cunningly woven net of fiction and lose their reality. Nothing is false, yet nothing is true.

No doubt a limitless future awaits this blurring of the truth, these halftone lies. What marvels of ingenuity lie ahead—careers for simulation specialists, perhaps, demented court cases at which only false testimony (all of it "real," in other words filmed) would be heard, or even TV games along the lines of: what is false in the historical scenes we are about to show you?

To these dubious methods can be added the techniques of so-called virtual or synthetic images—images which no longer depict reality but are a mathematical construct, born of a concept. This blurring of the truth can only get worse.

In the process our history, our memory, our everyday life, our relationship with things will lose all sharpness (if indeed everything in so-called real life is clear and sharp).

Examples abound, not of flagrant lying, as in the Bloch case, but of barely perceptible distortion. A TV news program broadcasts a brief report on a political rally at election time. The creators of the report must first isolate the words they intend to use from speeches made at the rally. This first choice is significant, for it inevitably loads the scales one way or another, the more so because speakers do not express themselves in public the way they would in a TV interview. Carried by the emotion of crowds that already share their views, they let themselves go; they wax eloquent and even bombastic. They raise their voices, wave their arms—hustings theatrics that are sure to look exaggerated and often ridiculous on the small screen, for television is an exercise in intimacy. All politicians are familiar with this double standard governing their public utterances, but very few master it.

And there is something subtler, more hidden. For the same political meeting the report will show a few frames, as tradition requires, of the listening audience. If the shots are of young, beautiful, eager-eyed, passionately applauding women (some political groups hire carefully selected walk-ons), the impression will be favorable. If, however, the spectators are dull-looking, or spectacularly ugly, the kind you see at every meeting, it will be bad news for the politician; a shadow will darken the report of the rally.

An alert spectator can tell from the producer's choices whether he is for or against the political party he is covering on a particular day. Yet to all appearances the producer has simply done his job. He has not distorted reality, he has selected fragments of it.

As in cinema.

Sometimes it is enough to be forewarned, to have a lucid grasp of the language of film, for every TV news program to become an interesting decoding exercise. We can then look with new eyes at the images that bombard us (nobody ever wholly escapes them), anticipating blind alleys, technical tricks, omissions. Our habitual passivity can give way to wakefulness, to curiosity, to a critical eye. A necessary, salutary attitude and—doubtless for that very reason—a perpetually threatened one.

But how many people will take the trouble, or are informed enough, to open their eyes, to see differently? Most of the time we stare supine and dullwitted at the image we are shown and the sound we are made to hear: dull and unreacting. Sometimes we hear that these are "exclusive" pictures—meaning that they have been acquired as a result of *sub rosa* deals and fees higher than the competition could afford. We are being tempted with promises of horrors.

After one railroad disaster I even heard a reporter say, "With luck, we will be able to show you footage of this horrible accident later on in the program."

An unhappy choice of words, no doubt. Every professional announcer is to some degree an actor. His face tells us at once whether the day's news will be funereal or jolly. He can hardly smile while reporting an assassination, an oil spill, or the defeat of the national team. For years now, the news has been a show, and the chief aim is basically entertainment. The last thing a network wants is for viewers to hunt for better news on some other channel.

Worse still, we know that in all wars, above all during street battles in cities, combatants are stimulated by the camera's presence. They will readily offer to go to the corner and loose off a burst of live ammunition for a reporter. So even some of these pictures are fakes. Volker Schlöndorff reports that in Beirut, while shooting *Die Fälschung (Circle of Deceit),* soldiers he had hired as extras offered to fire from a window and kill—at random—some passersby out in the street.

So the realistic power of motion photography can be deceptive. Will our descendants, even the most vigilant of them, always be able to tell genuine "live" news pictures from organized deception of the kind that characterizes propaganda films, from "simulations" in which actors and real-life characters are often clumsily confused, from blockbuster shows built up around a real event (like the Gulf War) which can strip it of all reality, or from unabashed studio reconstructions like those of Georges Méliès or of new-style "telejournalism"?

It is far from certain. This blurring of genres, already a staple of TV news programs, seems likely to insinuate itself soon enough into history proper. We already have programs calling themselves "historical" and making lavish use of "historical" films to illustrate the events they record. We are shown scenes from antiquity or the Middle Ages as if they were "live" news footage. We see Napoleon with Marlon Brando's profile, Joan of Arc with Ingrid Bergman's face and broad shoulders (and of course both speak English). Why not, after all? News reporting is regularly distorted and dishonest, so why not summon fiction to the rescue? If the film's labor of reconstruction is well done, avoiding known pitfalls (such as the gleam of stirrups in Bible stories or visible stocking seams on Pharaoh's daughters), the resulting visualization of history can not only be charming but can help us—via attitudes, play, actions, and even sounds— draw closer to the past. If we want to know exactly what a medieval peasant was thinking as he plowed the land, and how hard it was, it is sometimes enough to put a period implement into an actor's hands and ask him to perform the task. The implement dictates his posture and molds his movements. By gripping it and attacking the soil, he is already traveling in time.

What is valid for one man is just as valid for a group. To show us a great pyramid under construction in *Land of the Pharaohs*, set designer Alexandre Trauner had to tackle problems comparable to those confronting ancient

Egyptian builders. We should acknowledge his effort, his concern for the truth.

And then there are the films that straightforwardly reveal the lives of Abraham Lincoln, Gandhi, or Stalin, or above all Chaplin; in other words, people close enough to us for an accurate iconography, even photos and film footage, to be available.

Here fiction gets ambitious. A carefully made-up actor incarnates the great figure (there have been a good hundred Hitlers already, and the game has barely begun), the whole aim apparently being for the original and the replica to be interchangeable in a century or two. With Stalin, thanks to Soviet makeup artistry, telling the difference is already tricky. What will it be for our grand-children?

It's the inevitable triumph of historical fiction.

Like it or not, accept it or not, our vision of the past and perhaps even our sense of history now flow chiefly through film. There is no escaping it. Cinematic images write themselves into us without our knowledge, like masks placed over past centuries. Little by little they replace the older official versions—the great battle pan-oramas, official portraits of monarchs and dignitaries, cel-ebrated scenes, the long procession of lofty lies that once helped form our notions of history.

So one lie replaces another.

Today we are so overloaded with images of the past (true, half-true, or false) that the forest is lost for the trees, and some of film's technical shortcomings have a heavy impact on our basic perception of history. The absence of smell, for example. Historians all tell us, with great conviction, that the past stank, in the cities at any rate. In fact it stank most foully. But these foul smells—sweat, excrement, fetid air, decomposition—are almost impossible for us to imagine, to feel. Film, like an invisible screen between reality and ourselves, has vetoed it. Film has sweetened history, sanitized and dry-cleaned it, and all because of a simple technical deficiency.

And what producer would dare sell audiences tickets to a smelly auditorium?

Photography's power to convince is enhanced, as has often been pointed out, by the physical conditions—silence and darkness—in which films are shown. Spectators are away from their homes in strange surroundings, among unknown neighbors they will probably never see again. Like the chained men in Plato's cave, who see moving shadows and take them for reality, they too see pictures they call real as they sit motionless in the dark.

Seduced yet again (and astonished as well, for we vaguely remember that all this was made possible by our own technical ingenuity), our mind seeks only to surrender, to be duped, bluffed. Doubting Thomas again. We see, therefore we believe.

Some scientists insist that seeing is separating. No *vision* of totality is conceivable. To see, to be sure of seeing, you must differentiate the object beheld from all that surrounds and interferes with it. From the scientific standpoint, seeing is a technique and a subterfuge. All vision is relative and necessarily incomplete, since our eyes evolved in response to the light of the sun and thus can see only images born of the sun. The atom of the sun speaks the language of light to the atom of the eye. And our eye sees nothing else: it sees neither infrared nor ultraviolet rays nor several other kinds of cosmic rays. If we wish to see those, we must make ourselves other "eyes."

Film is of course the arch-separator. The borders of the screen are geometrically drawn, clean-cut. All around them is shadow. There is what is on the screen —a bombardment of organized photons—and what is not on the screen—the blurred, the dark, the undiscerned, the invisible. And even within that luminous squared-off space, only the sharp images are visible, those that are in focus; all the others are hazy, and our eye simply passes over them.

Thus, within this cordoned-off space, on the screen itself, technology can introduce an added separation by playing light against shade, sharp against hazy. The center of the square is where the invisible finger is pointing. Look only at what I choose to show you.

Time also separates. For the duration of the film, it briefly isolates a group of people from the rest of the world. As if, escaping life's turbulence for the space of two hours, the audience could forget time, could stop growing old. The modern cave shelters us from the oldest of evils.

And within this frozen time is another separation, created by silence. For two hours we will not speak, except in hushed tones, and like us, our neighbors in the audience will respect this vow of temporary silence. Only the photons beamed over our heads will express themselves. Only they will exist.

63

To this traditional separation, which we experience in the blackness of the auditorium, and which constantly reinforces the realistic power of photography, television has added considerable technical modifications. These change our relationship with the reality offered us. The first casualty was the luminous beam that once emanated from the back of the auditorium and passed with its cargo of living images through the dust-laden air above our heads. The image now comes to us head-on; we confront it directly. And the picture is smaller, so we dominate it rather than feel dwarfed by it.

The TV screen is still a finite surface, but darkness no longer reigns: visible all around us are everyday objects, books, chairs; the phone rings; we get up for a glass of something; we chat. In this less dark zone, where we might even have left lights on, other images and other sounds discreetly compete with the television. Farewell the monkish seclusion of the movie theatre. Reality, with its subtleties and temptations, settles in. We are at home.

But there is more: television keeps programs coming as rapidly as possible, one after the other, with just one rule: STAY WITH US. If we want to separate a film *in time*, isolate it from what precedes and follows it, we must act. Otherwise we will stumble, without missing a beat, into a commercial, a sports program, or a news roundup, in which real images blend dangerously with manufactured ones. How many times, still tearful over something just witnessed, have we not had our emotion brutally shattered by the irruption of mindless music or a ludicrous image?

Memory, like sight, is a matter of separation, of differentiation. We really remember only what we have singled out. If we want the recollection to endure, we have to protect it from contamination-by-confusion. Television, which continually mixes its genres and puts everything on the same plane (no announcer is ever going to tell us, "Don't watch what's coming, it really isn't worth it"), eliminates such demarcation. That is why it is first and foremost a device for inducing oblivion. By not allowing us to differentiate, it numbs our memory, because it mixes everything together, the serious and the trivial, the imaginary and real. We could almost say that television's role is to make us forget films, perhaps even forget life.

Watching TV, we are at once less fascinated and more distracted than at the cinema, as well as less discerning. Films we see again at home often look better than they did in the movie house. Our critical spirit dozes. After all, we haven't left home, we haven't paid (at least not obviously), and we have the permanent option of changing channels, and even of turning off the set. We have power over this device. To get it we spent money. It is therefore at our service. So our nature persuades us—just as we almost always sing the virtues of our own car—that it was a bargain.

Women are less scared of snakes on television than on the cinema screen. Something bland and reassuring has insinuated itself between us and reality. All effects are muted. The filmed object's power of conviction fades. The repetitious mediocrity of many TV series— car chases, waving guns, family crises, heartbreaks— submerges us in such a flood of cliché, of devalued images and of commonplace sounds, that our eye and our brain stop watching and listening to them. It is impos-

sible to separate any of these images from the ones surrounding it. The flood of uniformity flows slowly across
our retina without ever touching us.

Was the Romanian cameraman who filmed the trial,
execution, and burial of the Ceauşescus (an unforgettable
event in the history of television as well as of Romania)
aware of this danger? The extraordinary insistence with
which he dwelt on the dead faces, the riddled clothes,
the seeping blood, and five days later the swollen-
featured corpses emerging from the morgue to be loaded
onto hearses—everything seemed to tell us (in addition
to the clearly sacrificial aspect of the affair): take a good
look, it's them, it's really them, don't forget, never forget.

Every day we hear music that was deliberately composed not to be listened to. Music for elevators, waiting
rooms, restaurants, airports, supermarkets, a sonic background our body distractedly registers, without paying it
heed, sometimes against its will. Muzak is a syrup designed to blot out the world's real noises, perhaps to
reassure us, most certainly to lull us to sleep. Similarly,
particularly on television (quite unlike what happened
with the Ceauşescus), we live with images most as-
suredly designed not to be looked at. Seen, perhaps, but
not looked at.

Such images (we should find a name for them) fulfill
the same function as Muzak. They draw a veil between
us and reality; they hide the world from us. A police
series featuring injury-proof cops makes a total travesty
of the reality of crime and the real work of the police. It
is as if a whole city were masked. By their very ordinari-

ness, these ordinary images hide what they claim to depict. Without realizing it, we become habituated to this false world; it makes us see the city we live in as if it were wearing makeup. We no longer even see it—to the point where real violence, everyday violence, seems to us clumsy, incoherent, badly timed. Unprepared for the encounter, we stare in surprise. We have trouble believing it.

In some cases, film actually blinds us to who we are, to our country and our culture. Quite often in France suspects hauled into police stations ask to see an "attorney." They use the English word, behaving as if they were in a film. Ignorant of French judicial practice, they observe American law and procedure. One reality drives away another. And here too, error wins out.

What about variety shows, where the rule is for everyone to smile as toothily as possible? Or programs supposedly for the young—and here I have a particular Brazilian show in mind—which show beautiful women, generally blonde and miniskirted, mobbed by packs of children of every color? These programs seem to be on daily, and for hours on end they project an image of the world that is diametrically opposed to the daily life of those same children, who will be back on their mean streets once the broadcast is over.

What is the point? To make real life disappear? To ward off the world?

In the images we receive, everything becomes more and more like everything else. It is hard to surprise or unsettle us. There we sit, slumped and heavy-lidded. Images move deceptively before our half-closed eyes, and we think we are looking at them. They appear to mesmerize, but in fact they do not interest us. Every kind of joy and horror can come into our homes without disturbing us. We drink tea, we even consume hearty meals as we watch scenes of desolation and famine. In a sense, none of it affects us. The TV set transforms every apartment into a little fortress. If the set is on, it means all is well. Peace and order reign. The sad news we are seeing comes from elsewhere, from another country, another planet.

Basically, television is not of this world.

Here again we see the astonishing speed with which the first phase of cinema history has played itself out. As the aesthetic revolution gathered momentum, the spectator's attitude also changed radically, in just two or three generations. Those who stiffened in fear in their seats at the image of an oncoming train have become lumpish, unfeeling couch potatoes, reacting with the same bovine indifference to hours of glittering extravaganza as to hard-hitting news reports.

Images come and go. They flow over us, and our hides grow thicker.

And what exactly are these images for? We aren't sure. No one has ever bothered to tell us. Do we get to know each other better, to be better neighbors? What a joke! To make a little money, yes certainly; to kill time; but also to be like everyone else. Who today does not believe he lives in the "image civilization"? People tell us so, over and over, and we repeat it. We are permanently lapped around by images, at home, in the street, in subways and cars; they even build walls of images, and soon holography will give us houses and buildings of images. A planet of images. Images that move, talk, make noises. Images that obliterate (but do nothing to cure) our sense of solitude.

Yet we do not see them. Their sheer numbers and mediocrity prevent it. And as image has piled upon image (why did we call all this piling-up civilization?), reality has crumbled away. There is widespread talk of the disappearance of the image, drowned in its own superabundance. It could be that our world, more and more seen, is less and less understood.

It may be advisable when making films to be ignorant of the astonishing power that comes, or used to come, from the moving picture. Or, on the contrary, it may be advisable to be aware of it, to think about it. I don't know. Thoughtful filmmakers are not necessarily the best ones. They are dogged at every turn by the somewhat morbid temptations of analysis. On the other hand, it does no harm to stop from time to time, to think back, to ask yourself questions, to try to get organized—even if tomorrow everything blows apart.

This captivating power of the image obviously has its limits. We may be dulled, but the sentinels slumbering within us are still there. Foremost among them is boredom, good old boredom, that wonderful faculty of ours for losing interest, for instinctively refusing the mediocrity that is offered to us. Boredom is our faithful ally, our front-line natural defense, the one enemies have trouble hoodwinking.

How indeed could someone persuade us, once boredom has settled in, that we are not bored? A most difficult undertaking, for boredom-the-vigilant, which does not report to the brain, is utterly reliable and permanently on watch.

Boredom is pure, incorruptible, irrefutable. It is escorted by physical, visible signs, against which all arguments are vain. It begins with a feeling of lightness in the pit of the stomach, closely followed by rapid blinking, harbinger of yawns. Our attention wanders, our eyes cease to focus, we start to notice the people around us, the auditorium, the tempting lights discreetly marking the exit; we wonder what time it might be, we wonder which restaurant to head for after the show, we even think of tomorrow's schedule. Deep down we would like the film to speed up and reach a rapid conclusion, we would like to be an hour older. We try to list all the things we might have been able to do had we not chosen to come here; there is even anger at ourselves, at the reviewers or the friends who recommended this film.

We tend to overlook boredom, that shining virtue perhaps peculiar to our species. But we should rely on it, honor it, for it has shaken free of even the most secret and insidious of our mental processes; it appears unbidden, from nowhere, and invariably takes us by surprise. Well, what do you know, I'm bored! You notice it suddenly, like a nosebleed, like the urge to urinate. You can't wish it away. Boredom is conclusive: it is the irrefutable proof of the failure of what we are watching. No argument can budge it, nothing can cure it. It pierces the mask. It reveals the false behind what we thought was real.

Beside it stands another vigilant ally: "good taste," in other words our own taste, whose rightness we do not question. But of course as soon as we mention taste, everything becomes ambiguous. Even if what we are seeing seems hateful, there will always be someone to sing its praises. Nothing is less certain than taste, particularly the good variety. In film as elsewhere, we more often agree on dislikes than likes. Other people's enthusiasms always surprise us. We rarely share them.

We also know that at its birth virtually every masterpiece was rejected and reviled. It is almost a rule.

Every truly powerful work has to disturb. In fact, it is the sign of its power. I remember one day in Mexico bringing Buñuel the reviews of one of our films, *The Phantom of Liberty*, which had just come out in Paris. Buñuel took the clippings and read them. When I saw him again next day he looked gloomy. When I asked him why, he replied:

"For the first time in my life the reviews are all good. A bad sign."

A Buñuel who no longer disturbed, a pleasant, agreeable Buñuel, accepted by even the most respectable publications: inconceivable, intolerable, even disgraceful!

Luckily the film was shown at the New York Film Festival a few weeks later, and *Newsweek*'s reviewer savaged it. Luis's smile returned.

Unanimous approval is dangerous, and not just for Buñuel, for it may imply a conciliatory, soporific, and ultimately conventional work. Yet we seek approval most hungrily: on it hangs success, in other words the chance to make another film, and then perhaps another, and so on.

The defensive rampart of boredom, the rampart of the critical mind buttressed by our innate good taste, by our knowledge, by our cultural baggage ("I'm sure I've seen that shot somewhere else"). The querulous mind which so easily awakens the little judge slumbering in us all—that cold, ungenerous little judge, who has usually paid for his ticket and wants his money's worth. The second a hint of boredom deflects our attention from the screen, all these contradictory rumbles swirl over us as we sit there in the darkness. As long as the film holds us, nothing can touch us; we forget ourselves. But let the smallest thread snap—and sometimes it can be almost nothing, a clumsy phrase, a too-abrupt or too-slow gesture—and a thousand buried feelings surface: vague distaste, outright revulsion, a jealous twinge, resentment, sometimes even real shame just at being there, obscene guilt at having squandered any sum however small on an endeavor that suddenly looks pathetic.

Occasionally, too, there is an irrational dislike for an actor, because everything, or almost everything, in this domain is subjective. Unless they strike us as utterly neutral and boring, we feel instant sympathy or antipathy for actors. We want either to embrace or to strike or to flee them. And then there are whatever memories we might have of their former roles, which superimpose themselves like decals on their present images.

Every relationship between us and the actor, including our opinion of his work, must be transmitted affectively, through an unconscious rapport, an unspoken bond, of the kind we can have either with a family member or with an unknown person in the street. There is no rigid yardstick; even physical beauty, so decisive in the Hollywood of the 1930s, is no longer essential to the seducer. No one has ever been able to say what makes a star, why such and such a woman appears at a given moment to embody the desires and fears of her people, or even (depending on the commercial influence of the country she lives in) of other peoples, of all peoples. This affective connection—often very hard to bear, despite appearances, for the man or woman so elected—is pure mystery. It makes us swallow absurd stories because they are linked to a character who in our eyes can do no wrong. At other times it is the other way around: "If only he hadn't been in it! He ruined the whole thing for me!" No matter how great his talent, the actor we do not like destroys the story he tells. He prevents it from reaching us, and we blame him for it, sometimes to such an extent that if a certain actor is appearing in a film people recommend to me, I refuse to go.

A ridiculous attitude, but what can you do? The actor is a looking-glass in which it is impossible for everyone at once to recognize himself, no matter how flattering or seductive or moving the reflection thrown back. That reflection is always about us, or at least a part of us, and we all want to hold on to a certain image of ourselves. The identification phenomenon—that jewel of cinema, magical transference, the secret journey from one heart to another—is probably beyond rational explanation. It rattles too many imperfectly known parameters. When an actor's presence in a specific situation is all-powerful and irresistible, it sweeps everything before it, placates and blinds every conscience. The cinema draws us outside ourselves, actually slowing the movement of our hearts and lungs. It is difficult to go on talking about reality, since what we are doing is slipping inside an image, inside a body that is not ours, in a setting that is not ours.

Except on the rarest of occasions, the theatre does not really possess this ultimate weapon of great classical cinema. No matter how overwhelming, the stage actor remains himself, distinct from us. He speaks for us and suffers in our stead, not stripping us of ourselves the way film at its best can sometimes do. He remains a creature of flesh and blood, an animated mind, actually present before us. He may have other assets, often powerful ones, but he does not have the privilege (if it is one) of offering himself to us on-screen for a few hours of intimacy in a darkened auditorium. He is not a meticulously crafted image welcoming us with open arms into his world.

But with that said, and having paid passing tribute to the phenomenon, we are aware that this almost primitive bond is really a thing of the past. It belongs to the great reign of stars who magnified the everyday, bathing it in light (not for nothing were they *stars*), transforming every individual. Today too many arms are opened to welcome us. Too many idols, too many mirrors, too many new faces week after week. Too many voluptuous bodies in the harem. We fragment ourselves, we dissipate ourselves, and we are sent back to our solitude sooner than we used to be.

The now-threatened power to fascinate is reality in decline; images defeated by their very frequency: the television habit that has so swiftly transformed us has also led to a curious weakening of the filmed image.

A hegemony is under assault. It is a dangerous challenge, for cinema has a visceral need for this physical power to persuade, almost to mesmerize. If it loses this invisible link, it loses its essence, perhaps even its reason for being.

Everything in the cinema happens in ways diametrically opposed to the ways of the theatre, where reality is never perceived as true. However powerful a stage performance, we are still at the theatre: no Kabyle woman could imagine that actors really die on stage (after all, they even step forward to take their bow at the final curtain). We are touched only by a secondary reality, a reality of another order, easy to feel, difficult to describe.

Film can (or could at one time) literally possess us, in the double meaning of the word: it takes possession of us, dominates and manipulates us; and it also takes us in, deceives us. Here we have a paradox. Cinema makes use of illusion precisely because it is a sequence of photos set in motion, given sound, and then projected onto a determined area; precisely because it is an art rooted in reality, as if in exploiting illusion it acknowledges its inability to grasp and reconstruct that strange reality which even scientists hesitate to give a name.

Theatre is rooted in illusion, and makes no bones about it. Instead of trying to hide the fact, it often proclaims it, shouts it from the rooftops. We are in the theatre, the lights go down, we are about to see actors. No cheating there! And from this openly acknowledged

75

artifice, truth will either emerge or remain skulking in its lair.

But things are not always so simple. Forty or fifty years ago, overwhelmed and dazzled by the wonders of film, some theatre directors tried to fight back with the enemy's weapons and on the enemy's terrain. Like nineteenth-century painters striving to do work more real than photography, theatre directors fought back with a kind of hyperrealism.

This was truly a perversion of theatre. One French theatrical performance in the 1960s even advertised itself as being *"just like the movies."*

Which in itself makes no sense. Would we say the sea is fake if painted on a theatre backcloth and real if projected onto a screen? The screen sea is not the real sea either. It is a picture of the sea. Sometimes, on a theatre stage, a small puddle of real water is all you need to give a powerful impression, a realistic impression, of shoreline and open sea.

But in neither case can we speak of reality.

Once over the perverse urge to imitate a new form of expression in which the sky seemed the limit—as in painting after the shock of photography—the theatre soon found its direction again, but with a new boldness and power that stemmed directly from the life-or-death need to set itself apart from film.

Hence the astonishing freedom the theatre has forged for itself in the last thirty years, a period when the cinema was in its turn discovering, not without surprise, its new limits.

More easily and above all more naturally than cinema, the theatre can evoke and bring to life the audience's imaginings, its hidden visions. If at a given point in the *Mahabharata* an inspired actor says to us, "I see our elephants in the plain, their trunks severed, spewing blood," no spectator turns to look for elephants at the back of the auditorium. He sees them, if all goes well, somewhere inside himself. They appear independently of all realistic context, brought into being by the actor's fine performance and by the precise images it unveils for us, forces us to dig for and to see. They are images that all have something in common, yet all look different to each one of us.

This is a process that would be almost totally unacceptable in film. Film has to show the elephants. It has no choice: it is part of the contract each spectator made when he paid for his ticket. Indeed, special-effects teams will be assigned to create fake trunks spurting fake blood —no easy matter: in *Quest for Fire,* Jean-Jacques Arnaud had to disguise elephants as mammoths. He shudders at the memory.

In cinema the imagination is less alert, more passive. It relies on and believes in technique. It does its secret work only in slow motion, and in other areas. It expects the film to do the routine work. Not to show the stricken elephants would almost certainly trigger a frustration which would cost the film's creators and producers dearly, unless of course they made the elephants' absence an exercise in style, an experiment, for example making a film based on third-person stories. But in that case it might be advisable to warn the customers ahead of time.

When I began to write for the theatre twenty years ago, people around me said, "You're crazy, you're doing well in films, why do you want to work in theatre? The theatre's washed up, movies and TV are going to gobble everything up, soon there won't be any theatre left."

Some added, "Theatre is limited, narrow, convention-bound. In film you can show everything and do everything!"

I had no answer at the time, except perhaps that I felt a need to work in theatre and had no idea where that need came from. I wrote a first play that was a hit, a second that flopped. Being equally fond of both plays, like every author, I had no idea why they met such different receptions. I was puzzled. It was then I met Peter Brook. He led me off on a very long journey.

At about the same time cinema was treading water, after the surges of the New Wave and of films made in Italy, Germany, Brazil, and one or two other countries. Theatre, meanwhile, had been stood on its head. Everything was shattered. The rigid framework of the standard stage (which had inspired the cinema screen) burst wide open, as theatre invaded auditoriums and spilled into warehouses, railroad stations, trains, prisons. It moved from *two-room theatre* (clear-cut separation of performers and spectators) to *one-room theatre*, in which everyone occupies the same place on the same day to take part in the same experience and the same specific emotion.

Theatre—hitherto confined to a stage lit by footlights —was discovering the heady joys of space, of true space, the kind you share, in which you breathe together. In film, no matter how vast the horizon, space remains an illusion. It is only the image of space. Theatre, on the other hand, by invading untoward places, by exploiting the shifting subtleties of light, has learned how to multiply and transform its space, sometimes creating it out of a single gesture by an actor.

Far from disappearing, as the prophets of doom had foretold, the theatre, freed of the fatal urge to reproduce fleeting reality, today seems more vital than ever throughout the world. Indeed, it can seem that the higher you heap one pan of the scales with technological wonders—synthetic images, electronic cassettes, laser-read discs, satellites, high definition—the lower the other pan will sink under the weight of what I believe is the finest material—human material, the living material of the actor. We had believed theatre was threatened, yet it has won the day, swung the scales. All the more decisively, for by emerging from the confinement of classical theatrical space, theatre has learned how to travel. Clearly threatened by cinema's gift for the spectacular, it has suddenly become lighter, stripped itself of its former pomp, rediscovered a direct, real approach, even occasionally pushing the link with the audience's imagination to extreme limits.

In a production Peter Brook put on at the Bouffes du Nord in Paris in December 1989 (an adaptation of *Woza Albert,* a South African play by Mbongeni Ngema, Percy Mtwa, and Barney Simon), two French-speaking black actors, Mamadou Dioumé and Bakary Sangaré, played a whole series of South African characters, sometimes white, sometimes black. When they had to turn into whites, Peter simply asked them to pull a little tube of white cream from their pockets and daub a streak on their noses. Swiftly and openly done, it did not disguise the actors (who obviously remained black), but it permitted an extra level of complicity with the audience without in any way detracting from its laughter or its tears. Quite the contrary, in fact. In the original version of the same play, the two performers put on and took off a white nose as their roles demanded. And so forth. A thousand overt and visible tricks are permissible.

But who would risk them in film? Experiments of this kind have opened only narrow pathways, often interesting, but rapidly closing again. The cinema remains quite fundamentally a realistic medium. Whether in an auditorium or on a TV screen, it is still just that isolated rectangle made up of successive photos. And its legendary power ("you can show everything in cinema") has by the same token become its strange new weakness: "you *have to* show everything on film."

Yet film does not show everything. It struggles ceaselessly against its own condition, and one way or another, every great filmmaker was born from that struggle. The people who "do films" the way they would do anything else simply set up the camera at the likeliest-looking spot and film action that is basically a string of illusions and clumsy approximations. Working in a ready-made language to which they add nothing, they reiterate forms which are only thirty or forty years old but which already seem archaic to us. It is as if they had turned a blind eye to the essential matter, to the real struggle. Unable to cope with this hybrid reality, they resort to the facile, the uncontroversial.

At the other extreme, the filmmaker determined truly to express himself through film first of all confronts film's major obstacle, which is also its foremost weapon: the reality of the image. He seeks, he fights, he dares, and sometimes he even finds. He can distort that reality, like

F. W. Murnau in *Nosferatu,* or on the contrary pretend to respect it in order the more gently to mask it, like Jean Renoir in *Une Partie de Campagne.* He may proclaim and emphasize it, like Vittorio de Sica and Roberto Rossellini, or transfigure it, like Orson Welles and Federico Fellini. But every significant work has to go through this struggle. Otherwise, defeated in advance, the work becomes fuzzy, becomes one with the amorphousness in which we usually live. It lacks independent life; it vanishes the moment it appears.

In this inevitable, often obsessive, sometimes even insurmountable relationship with reality, cinema has turned to cheating in order to circumvent the obstacles reality raises. Some of its tricks occur so frequently that they are like a second reality slipped inside the first. We no longer—or hardly ever—notice them.

We know, for example, that in film a character always finds an unoccupied taxi ready to pick him up the second he needs it. On leaving the taxi a little later he pays the exact fare, never waiting for change, never even checking the meter.

On the phone (totally lost time, which is why good screenwriters avoid it), film characters always dial at top speed, dialing six figures instead of seven, or seven instead of eight. The person at the other end picks up at once, as if waiting by the phone for the call.

Still on the phone, employing a formula borrowed straight from between-the-wars theatre, the character on screen always repeats his unseen interlocutor's words: "How are you? Better? I'm so glad . . . And your wife? She's left you? Are you serious? She left with Maurice?" And so on.

In real life, of course, no one talks on the phone in this way.

And no one—or so we fervently hope—makes love the way they do in film. In the past, when a couple finally found themselves in bed together, the camera was polite enough (or perverse enough) to gaze discreetly at the curtains or the ceiling decoration, letting the lovers have at it off-camera. Today we show it all. We flaunt it. We require the unfortunate actors, often victims of mutual loathing, to pretend to love each other, to love each other physically and in a most intimate fashion in the presence of a good two-score highly attentive technicians.

The results are nearly always deplorable, and re-markably unconvincing. In so-called soft scenes (often called "erotic" to distinguish them from true pornogra-phy), when the male member is not shown in full erec-tion, penetration (off-camera) is always effected with astounding ease, apparently without the woman remov-ing her pants or the man his trousers, without a down-ward glance or fumbling helping hand, without a second's hesitation. Further, ecstasy occurs for both part-ners after barely a dozen reciprocal thrusts. Here too, as with phones and cabs, the accent is on haste. Thus to-day's films are a welter of premature ejaculations, unless, as in the theatre, these represent an experiment in style, in suggestion. But if so, why get down to the action at all? Everyone knows that the most erotically powerful images, the kind we have occasionally encountered in the cinema or elsewhere, most often stem from stimula-tion, from suggestion, from promise rather than perfor-mance. So why this mania for showing us badly made love? Nor is the demonstration any more convincing in hard or X-rated films. Here the depiction of lovemaking is actually even less honest, because it appears more real. They certainly seem to make wild and uninhibited love in these films, and in every conceivable position. In fact, that is all they do: one organ penetrates another, orgasm is visible. The man's in any case; its visibility is even part of the actor's contract, with ejaculation taking place on-screen, fully lit, with no receptacle in sight, to prove that the man's pleasure was not simulated. Hence the strange mania for coitus interruptus by hard-core studs who then ejaculate outside their partners.

But they do ejaculate. I have seen it, I cannot deny it, and Doubting Thomas would agree with me (adding his own shocked cries). Perhaps these are not ideal orgasms, but that is none of my business.

For the woman, on the other hand, the lie is total. Act-as-if is the watchword. Hard films give a new lease on life to the shameful tradition of beer-hall songs and what used to be called lurid novels, in which the good lover is a sort of blind and brutal stallion who makes love six or seven times a night and in which the woman—in any case a submissive creature—takes her pleasure at the same breakneck pace and with no hint of clitoral stimulation. Everything from moans to swoons is fake, utterly fake. And it sets a bad example, not for piffling moral reasons (which are none of my business) but quite simply because this particular lie could lead uninformed couples to believe that things happen and should happen that way, resulting in a totally mistaken notion of love.

In New York in the 1960s, I once sat in on the shooting of an X-rated movie. There was a man and two naked women in a Greenwich Village house. A small crew. A director and a cameraman. I spent ten minutes seated on a chair politely watching it all. You are very quickly struck by the everyday, joylessly professional, matter-of-fact tone: "Turn that way a bit, Lisa . . . Yes, a little more . . . Raise that knee a couple of inches . . . OK, keep going, keep going . . ."

Where is the pleasure in it? No one asks for love—but pleasure?

I thought that day of a remark by André Breton, in which he defined eroticism as "a sumptuous ceremony in an underground passageway."

That kind of film has betrayed us. What has it left us of ceremony, of sensuality, of somber subterfuge?

And what about realism? Made-to-order female orgasm is clearly a sham; furthermore, male orgasm does not happen as easily as people believe, despite appearances. In fact, everything in this repetitious and dully predictable sequence of staged routines is cut, spliced, and edited as for a film. The continuity essential to love disappears. The action is accelerated by tricks of cutting: we even hop fairly often from one face to the other, and there is no guarantee that the male member I see ejaculating in closeup is the same one I saw laboring away in a medium-close shot a moment ago. Mountains of premeditated trickery surround these naked bodies, which are supposed to be holding nothing back . . .

The same could be said about martial-arts films, and more generally about all film brawls, in which blows never really land and the illusion of violence comes from movement and especially from sound, from the noise of the blow tacked on later in the studio. Enormous portable killing machines fire off devastating projectiles. Their explosions make a terrifying but artificial din, often constructed of synthetic sounds. Bullets tear huge bloody holes in hostile chests. Never was anything of the kind seen in pictures of real war. And almost never in a real-life street fight does a man drop senseless from a single blow.

Some lies are by omission. For example, if a story does not call for the presence of children, a couple can live together for years and make love every day (and this rule has been in force since before the advent of the Pill) with no hint of offspring or discussion of the possibility.

Yet in other stories a man and woman meet, are attracted, make love just once, and the woman is pregnant.

In the cinema every activity is familiar and easy. Characters know how to swim, read, dance, ride, speak foreign languages. They always find a hotel room, and when they ring for the bellhop he appears at once. Cars start at the first try and the cavalry (almost) always arrives just in time. You shave without cutting yourself and smoke without getting sick. You urinate with extreme rarity—never mind the other, which you never do. Women wake up with their makeup on and their hair done. Travelers lug enormous suitcases with the greatest of ease. The same goes for a man carrying a woman in his arms: some thus burdened can climb several flights without faltering. When a character takes notes, or writes to dictation, he does it at dizzying speed, as fast as the person speaking. And when a young woman of quite intellectual aspect is brushed by love's wing, a true optical miracle occurs: she suddenly gives up wearing glasses without any apparent effect on her ability to read or write. The heroes of Westerns not only have inexhaustible ammunition in their guns, they also manage to bring down their foes at incredible distances, even though a revolver—as we all learn in the army—is wildly inaccurate beyond fifteen or twenty feet. Critically wounded men suddenly sit bolt upright in their hospital beds, rip out their intravenous tubes, and stalk outside to settle accounts.

Another constant: a man has just committed a crime; he escapes, gets to his hideout, and turns on the radio or TV. Invariably, at that very moment, the announcer is speaking of his crime and getaway.

And so it goes, on and on, each item accompanied by the hot breath of cliché. All these run-of-the-mill tricks, all these improbable acts that are nevertheless part of everyday cinema reality, have proliferated beyond belief in what we call "fantasy movies" (flying men, talking dogs, uncanny mental powers, aliens) and in adventure fiction, from Robin Hood to James Bond, in which a hero takes on the impossible and sweeps everything, even the laws of probability, before him. So much so that in French the expression *c'est du cinéma* soon came to mean "that's fake, that's bullshit." And when someone tries to dazzle you, promises more than he can deliver, the French say, *"Il fait son cinéma"*: meaning "He's feeding you a line."

And here the provisional paradox ends. Since its raw material is filmed reality, the cinema has had to cheat more often and more skillfully than other forms of expression. Daily exposed to the temptations of facility, it has invented countless new forms of lying. Behind its depiction of the attitudes and events of what it claims

86

to be everyday life, it often distorts feelings and ideas. Emboldened by laws of probability that are exclusively cinematographic ("this has to be true—I saw it at the movies"), it routinely depicts irrational conduct which nevertheless, from pure habit and inertia, seems normal to us. And yet at the same time it systematically rejects everything that in real life strikes us as unusual or preposterous. For we all have examples of real events, things which really happened to us or which we know to be true, but which we would never allow into one of our films. How many times do we say sadly of some real-life event, "That would never work in a screenplay." Coincidences, improbable happenings—the truth is not consistently convincing. We have always known that. Film, which so often ventures into the unreal, persistently forgoes a reality it finds too hard to swallow.

Greta Garbo is ushered into the office of businessman John Gilbert. Flawless as ever, face inscrutable, she takes the chair in front of him without even removing her coat.

This erotic scene is from a silent film, *A Woman of Affairs*, directed by Clarence Brown in 1929. The film, a hit in its day, has left no very memorable trail. But it might be interesting to recall today, with bare flesh everywhere, with ubiquitous penetration, how in that age of strict censorship the cinema cheated and invented in order to say everything without showing anything. In other words, how a resolutely unrealistic scene could acquire real power.

Garbo puts her hand on the arm of her chair. On the

hand is a ring decorated with a big dark stone. The ring is too big for her finger. The businessman, seated behind his desk, and already disturbed by the presence of his visitor (whom he has met before), notices this ring and says words that appear in a subtitle inset:

"Your ring is loose."

An exchange of glances. Then Garbo, still cold and aloof, replies (another inset, forcing the dialogue writer to the strictest economy):

"I've been told I'm like that ring—apt to fall."

The man looks at her and says nothing. He believes neither his eyes nor his ears. Did the woman wear this ring on purpose, just to provoke that remark and that reply? We have no idea—but we can dream. John Gilbert dreams too. A woman is sitting across from him, the woman is the peerless Greta Garbo, an actress at the top of her profession, known the world over, and this woman is hinting that she is apt to fall.

She rises slowly, removes her coat, just her coat, and in a dark suit, also sober and unexceptionable, she walks to a nearby couch and sits down. This couch, its shape and height carefully calculated, looks remarkably soft. Greta Garbo sinks into it and looks at the man. She is fully dressed. You cannot even see her knees.

Still seated behind his desk, John Gilbert looks back at her through glittering eyes lined with black makeup. Now he seems frightened, for he is faced with the inevitable, which is at the same time the unpredictable, the inconceivable. Fate has seated itself on the couch. Who would have thought it just five minutes ago? A woman of whom you and I would not even have dreamed, a woman no man touches, is sitting there in your office, on your couch, and telling you (another subtitle) that she loves you.

A minute to shatter a man's day, perhaps his life.

Gilbert rises in turn, removing neither tie nor shoes. Love here operates in the absolute, without everyday constraints, without the almost invariably absurd need to lower one's trousers.

He approaches the couch and sits beside the woman. They exchange a few glances and two more subtitles. Their feelings are no longer in doubt. They are soon in one another's arms. Then Garbo falls back on the couch, drawing the man down as she sinks. And just as quickly, the camera leaves them. It follows Garbo's hand, which slips from couch to floor. The ring slowly slips from her finger and falls soundlessly to the rug. Silence, palpable even in a silent film.

This scene, from an unambitious melodrama, is in appearance ordinary enough, with the unseen and the unspoken triumphing at every step, with not even one bone for the censor to pick. Yet the scene suggests, evokes, pushes open all the right doors within us. Everything in it is visible and comprehensible, even the maneuvering, even the possibility of deceit.

But ordinary reality has been eliminated. Nobody wonders where the bathroom is, or if a secretary will appear without warning. All these reasonable questions no longer count. What counts is the scene's style, that notion of the ring and all the suggestions that follow upon it. Its authors hope that this idea has a strong enough hold for the audience not to ask itself the other questions, the practical questions.

In this scene love, or at any rate a form of love, has

virtually been invented. It will eventually give birth to all the clichés—the camera panning at the crucial moment to the crackling wood fire, to toppling shoes, to clothing tossed to the rug, to the music from a record player—but for the period, 1929, the characters' movements retain all their freshness, all the insolence of invention.

The scene from *A Woman of Affairs*, duly submitted to the censors, could be characterized as "stopping this side of reality." And the constraints imposed by censorship were, of course, the direct source of the scene's strength.

It was one way of proceeding, one way of handling a reality both taboo and difficult to convey, downplaying matters politely and by the rules—which can also sometimes mean disaster. In Franco's Spain it was forbidden to mention adultery on-screen. A wife could not have a lover, nor a man a mistress. So in Spanish versions of foreign films these characters were renamed brothers and sisters, which led to highly alarming scenes. In *Back Street*, Charles Boyer wonders tearfully if he dares run away with his sister. Incest, in the name of family values, had entered Iberian cinemas.

And so it goes. The effects of censorship have often been perverse.

At the opposite pole there have been a few—a very few—who dreamed of making the screen explode, destroying paradox, going beyond the barriers technology imposes on our perceptions.

One is Buñuel. In one of his very rare lectures, at the University of Mexico in 1953, he said:

"The screen's white eyelid would have only to reflect the light peculiar to it and we could blow up the universe. . . . Film is a magnificent and dangerous weapon if it is wielded by a free mind. It is the finest instrument we know for expressing the world of dreams, of feeling, of instinct. The mechanism that creates cinematographic images is, by its very function, the form of human expression most closely resembling the work of the mind during sleep. Film seems to be an involuntary imitation of dream . . . the darkness that gradually invades the auditorium is the equivalent of closing our eyes. It is the moment when the nightly incursion into the unconscious begins on the screen and deep inside man. As in dream, images appear and disappear in 'dissolves,' and time and space become flexible, contracting or expanding at will. Chronological order and relative duration no longer correspond to reality. . . ."

On the verge of this plunge into the unconscious, which is not only the unseen but the unknown, the ground seems ripe for hallucination, for surpassing and forgetting the self (which is the condition for discovery of self), for the gentle or ungentle overturning of barriers. And it happens sometimes without warning. At the end of *Rosemary's Baby*, directed by Roman Polanski, many spectators *saw* the monstrous child, the Devil's spawn, in his crib. Some, I remember, even described him in detail. And yet that image does not occur, not even fleetingly, anywhere in the film. Polanski never filmed it. His characters lean over the crib, look at the baby, talk about him. Our deep-seated perception, if we are among those who see the young monster, here goes further than the film itself: it opens up, turns itself inside out, and finally sees the unseeable.

The end of Buñuel's *Belle de Jour* brought a similar surprise. This is a truly inexplicable scene, halfway between reality and fantasy, in which the heroine Séverine's conflicts seem suddenly to be resolved. Her husband, sitting paralyzed in a wheelchair, abruptly rises as if cured, whereupon a tear (of forgiveness?) runs down his cheek. He walks smiling toward his wife, who watches him and seems happy. They go together to the window. Outside, an empty coach crosses the autumn landscape, doubtless carrying the heroine's dangerous fantasies off to an unknown destination.

But what reality are we in, what stage of the story have we reached? Neither Buñuel nor I nor the actors could say. Every attempt to explain struck us as arrogant, disastrous. During shooting, Buñuel gave the performers only elementary physical instructions; he made no attempt to penetrate the story's various psychological layers, as if he wished to respect the mystery for its own sake, to work in the same mists as the actors. It was a scene dreamed up in one evening after fairly exhaustive research, a scene which so moved Luis as it was being filmed that tears came to his eyes when he described it. But afterward we discussed it very little. When you are lucky enough to encounter true mystery, Buñuel often said, you must respect it. And dissecting mystery is like violating a child.

When the film came out a great many women spoke to us of the baby they had *seen* during this sequence. Yet another baby. But what baby? There is no baby here, or in any other scene in the film. Yet some female spectators swore they remembered an infant crying. Luis admittedly inserted a cat's mewing into the soundtrack to help recall an earlier scene. This mewing gave birth to recollections of a baby's cries, then of the baby itself, absent but still visible to these women. Their secret desires (but again, it is not for me to interpret motives) were speaking loud and clear. The wall was shattered for a few seconds, the paradox resolved.

In the same film a hefty Korean, a passing visitor at Madame Anaïs's modern brothel, shows the ladies the inside of a little box he intends to use. We do not see what the box contains, but we hear a small indefinable sound inside it. Horrified, two of the girls refuse. Séverine smiles and agrees, and goes into a bedroom with the Korean and his box.

Probably more than a thousand times over the past twenty years, I have been asked what was in that box. I did not know what to say, because of course we never knew. It stood for everyone's secret desire, everyone's unnameable perversion. I would answer as best I could, jokingly. People would say: it was a snake, or a particular instrument shaped this or that way, and so forth. As usual, each answer diminished the question, which to me (with Asia's help) seemed rather open, like a Zen question.

One day a stranger phoned and out of the blue asked me at what period of my life I had lived in Laos. Never, I told him. And Luis Buñuel? Neither had he. Are you sure? Absolutely sure.

"In that case," the stranger said, "how did you come to put an old Laotian custom into *Belle de Jour*?"

"Which one?"

"Why, the box the customer brings in!"

"You know what was in the box?"

"Of course."

"Tell me, quick!"

Most obligingly, and with many details, the man told me that in the old days certain refined Laotian ladies would truss a large beetle with a thin gold chain and set it on their clitoris during the act of love. The wriggling of the creature's many legs induced an indescribable degree of added pleasure. The custom, added the stranger, had in all likelihood been lost in the political and military disasters that had befallen Southeast Asia—but here it was, astonishingly resurrected in a French film.

I thanked him and hung up.

For a few days this story amused me and I repeated it to people. But I soon realized that it had turned an open highway into a blind alley. This coincidence—supposing the story to be true—contributed nothing to the film and took something away from it. The indefinable was better than the specific, however exotic. Buñuel, moreover, dreamed of slipping a few items of false information into all his films, as if briefly to undermine and divert the course of geography and history; true reality irked him like a tight corset.

It was probably in his last film, *That Obscure Object of Desire*, shot in 1977, that he pulled off his most astonishing feat of legerdemain. While writing the screenplay, we considered giving the role of the elusive young woman (Conchita) to two different actresses, turn by turn, without warning, without announcing or stressing the feat. We felt that certain scenes were better suited to an elegant and rather aloof woman, while others seemed written for an earthier actress, someone forthright—and able to dance flamenco.

In fact, we spent a half-day assigning scenes to each one, without changing a line of the script, and of course without having the other characters notice these sudden substitutions.

At the end of the day, though, Buñuel decided it was all an idle whim. He dropped the idea, and began shooting in the most orthodox fashion, with just one actress. But he was unable to direct her satisfactorily. Worried, unhappy with the results of the first few days' work, he showed the early rushes to Serge Silberman, the producer, and told him disconsolately that he could not make the film.

This took place in a bar one evening in Madrid. Suddenly, during a lull, doubtless remembering our earlier and short-lived experiment, Luis asked Silberman, "Do you believe there is one woman who could be all women?"

Silberman quickly understood what was being suggested, and agreed to have two actresses play Conchita.

This decision called into question the time-honored notion of identification of actor with character. Although this has sometimes happened in theatre (Hamlet played by three different actors in the same performance, for example), we knew of no such instance in the history of film. Hence a definite risk, which Silberman unhesitatingly accepted.

A few weeks later shooting resumed in Paris with two actresses playing Conchita, the Spanish Angela Molina and the French Carole Bouquet. Two details: their clothes were similar, and more important, they were dubbed by the same voice.

But their faces, their figures, their acting style remained noticeably different, even though both were dark-haired. Yet—and here is the mystery—many spectators failed to notice that the part was played by two different actresses. One of my friends, normally most attentive, told me that in his view there was "something odd" about Conchita, although he could not put his finger on it. Some people, of course, knew beforehand, having read about it; others duly noticed the substitution. But a good half of the spectators saw nothing. A post-screening poll in an American university indicated that seventy percent of the students had not spotted the difference.

That was indeed an example—it still astounds me today—of mild but enduring hallucination. Should we wonder at it, or should we be concerned? It shows the degree to which our eyes can remain unseeing for more than an hour and a half as a result of the almost frightening power of our habits of perception, our secret rejection of the out-of-the-ordinary, of all that upsets and disconcerts.

Film: a power that placates reality.

Such examples of hijacking are rare. As Buñuel himself said, "We can sleep easy for now." The opportunity to wake from—or rather to go beyond—our hypnotic sleep, to set in motion what is most secret in us, what weighs heaviest, what is hardest to acknowledge: such opportunities are for the moment almost lost. Nearly every film we see seems chained to reality. For a thousand reasons, most of them supposedly commercial, they act as if. They reconstruct. Such is cinema: chained to what it shows us, so that we cannot follow Cézanne's advice and "unite women's curves with the shoulders of hills." We would have to have a special cinema, one that nobody could define, one that might seem to save appearances, to save the surface, the more insidiously to penetrate the heart . . . Or the absolute opposite: the kind of cinema which if it dared nothing else would dare to go beyond labels. But I know I am flirting here with utopianism and taking the easy way out—wishing for something new. And what about habits of thinking? And security? And money worries, those hidden censors?

In any case, dreaming of a kind of cinema that does not yet exist (even though we might be carrying it in embryo) means not reducing it to an investigation into form. It means trying to open more dangerous trapdoors. It means accepting ahead of time one's stake in a game whose rules one does not know. It means touching secret mechanisms we are not sure we can slow or stop once they are in motion. And whatever else, it means knowing from the start that reality will resist us with all its might.

Nineteen years' collaboration with Buñuel, the very model of a modern *Su(pe)rr*ealist, taught me on a daily basis how incredibly hard it is for us to catch reality napping. To return to *Belle de Jour*: Luis did not want the audience to see or hear any difference between the supposed real life and the fantasies of Séverine, the young middle-class woman who spends her afternoons at a brothel. Indeed, the whole film seems to say there is no difference, that the imagined life is as real as the other, and that the life we believe to be real can at any given moment be improbable, absurd, abnormal, per-verse, carried to extremes by our secret desires.

One of Séverine's fantasies, one of her imaginings, shows her going to a country chateau where a middle-

97

aged aristocrat asks her to lie in a coffin for a strange, probably masturbatory, and incidentally authentic ceremony (like all the film's fantasies, it was told to us). This scene follows the visit by the duke's manservant to the brothel to select a girl. The manservant's appearance gave the whole chateau scene a feel of unarguable reality, which was the opposite of what we intended. During editing Luis cut out the manservant scene in order to stress the dream quality of the visit to the chateau. Apparently in vain. For most spectators the scene remained real.

Most of the time we are defeated by reality, which is stronger and more cunning than we are. We sometimes try to make room for those who would like to slip their dreams in next to ours. Nothing could be more disappointing. When Buñuel introduced a bear into the stately home in *The Exterminating Angel*, critics sought in it an allegory of Soviet Russia, and in the sheep at the end, an obvious image of subject peoples. When in *The Discreet Charm of the Bourgeoisie* we sent our characters on foot down a road leading nowhere, people asked us where they were going. Worse still, some spectators insisted that they were dead, and doomed like the Wandering Jew to eternal roaming.

All those—and they are, alas, many—who reject dreams or detours or the smallest sidestep simply slam the door in our faces. So we seek refuge in what we can see and touch. The visible reassures us. Everything we can give a shape to reassures us. Even if that shape is eccentric, it still comes from our hands, we have fashioned it. What disturbs has no defined shape, no shape we could reproduce however intelligently we tried; and yet we feel it move and breathe, kicking us, sometimes biting us. Cinema, apparently intended for long descents into all such chasms, in fact usually steers clear of them —unless it confines itself to eliciting from them decorative, surprising, or pleasing effects. After all, why not? we say to ourselves. Why pound on that door which may lead nowhere, and which in any case no one has asked us to open? We stay on the beaten track. We support ourselves with both hands against the walls that both hem us in and guide our steps. Cinema is still pushing along this treacherous corridor, and perhaps will long go on doing so.

All festivalgoers know this strange and somewhat disturbing feeling: after sitting through two or three consecutive films, at the Cannes Festival for example, we emerge somewhat dazed, somewhat lost. The palm trees on La Croisette, the sea, the strollers, all suddenly seem singularly unreal. We have left true reality behind in the auditorium, a confused welter of the images that survive of the day's handful of films. Threatened with instant oblivion, this daily-repeated chaos will nevertheless be all our memories consent to harvest and hoard from this day's viewing. We have not really been living. Seated in the gloom, we have quit our bodies, our minds, and perhaps even our souls; we have remained long separated from ourselves, all in the interests of this imperious (but already muddled) sequence of sounds and images that have enveloped, drained, and destroyed us.

What happens in the course of one day also happens over a longer period: a month, a year, a whole slice of our lives. With the exception of outstanding films—which we usually see again from time to time—most melt into an ill-defined magma that is doubtless deposited in some lazy area of our brain. There are films seen in childhood and on vacation, films from student days, films seen with our spouses, films seen in New York and elsewhere: a private and personal system of classification for each individual. In another book I have written about my memories of films seen in a small garrison town in Algeria in 1960, during what we then called "pacification" and now call a war. For over a year I went to the cinema there three times a week, and I recall only two or three titles. The others have blurred together. They constitute one single film, in which incoherence reigns. Pirates, cowboys, and medieval knights mill in disorganized combat. I can see galloping horses—but are they off to storm a fort in New Mexico or a fortress in Mesopotamia? I do not recall. The cinema—that cinema—demanded too much of my memory, which has now taken its revenge.

What will remain to us of the endless tapestry of images unwinding before our eyes?

In diverse guises, the filmed image has launched a methodical invasion which is meeting no resistance. The most traditional of societies, those we used to consider the best insulated, have no antidote to the videocassette. They were seduced at the first caress. A colored picture that moves and makes sounds: for them, as for us, it is irresistible. Amazon Indians, still almost naked (except for the missionary-mandated shorts), deftly operate video cameras. In the market stalls of Africa and New

Zealand, in the farthest recesses of Central Asia, all the world's films are available. Even in Iran, where American products are almost uniformly forbidden, Hollywood videocassettes are smuggled across the frontiers. An irresistible invasion.

Is this deplorable? Or is it a good thing? I don't know. Nobody knows. But that is how it is, and nothing will change it. Not at once, anyway. We can speculate that the century may gradually jettison useless images in order to rediscover or discover something else. But it is a hollow dream. For now, and for a long time to come, the image has prevailed. For better and for worse. Maybe this long river will flow on without drowning us, like lustral water, bringing in its passage only a distraction, a respite from a too-arduous existence, an isolated moment, benign, soothing, and at once forgotten. Time wasted, perhaps, but at least during that time no one has fought, no one has killed, no one has ill-used the earth. The image lulls and paralyzes. There are those who might prefer the other.

Perhaps the real danger in this saturation-by-image that everyone is talking about (generally with alarm) lies in the disappearance, pure and simple, of what we used to consider reality. There is the danger that reiterated images of the world will ultimately replace the world. The danger that a popularized and universally disseminated cinema may cut us off, with no hope of return, from whatever remains of reality. That in a world we know is doomed to disappear (and perhaps sooner than we think) we might find temporary refuge in representation of that world. When all the trees are dead, a decorator friend recently told me, they will manufacture more in film studios. There, water will flow crystal-clear, and birds will sing.

Three years ago I saw an ominous documentary on TV. Patients from Chernobyl, Russians who had been exposed to severe radiation, sat before a screen in a small projection room. Their bodies were damaged, but so were their minds. What lesions had they suffered? We were not told. Perhaps no one knew.

As they sat there, expressions dull, heads lolling, these motionless men were shown still-shots of nature, nature in all its glory, blue, pine-fringed sea, tranquil woodland, a cool mountain stream—a few of the wonders menaced by the catastrophe that had struck them down. According to the voice-over, doctors hoped that this visual stimulus might awaken what was still alive in their brains.

Perhaps one day we will be like those diminished, misshapen men, huddled for refuge in some shelter. That time will come, and perhaps many alive today will see it. But no need to worry: we will possess enough information by then to remember the old life and build facsimiles of it. We are already doing so. In some parts of France they are already putting up fake villages, carefully reconstructing what was everyday life to me when I was a child, and people come to visit, to gape at this object of curiosity. Not even one lifetime has gone by, and already my childhood is in a museum. Which means it has vanished.

There is the danger of losing touch with things and people without anyone even noticing. The danger of going more and more often and more and more mechanically through the looking-glass to the place where there are still tall trees (of painted cement, on studio lots) and naked Indians (made-up, unionized extras).

There is the danger of finding this journey pleasant and even exhilarating, since in that world (as the old Kabyle woman failed to understand) even death is artificial.

The danger of fleeing for a long time, perhaps with no chance of getting back.

The danger, too, that by looking at this world of ours we may cease to see it.

TIME DISSECTED

In 1972 a retired Los Angeles film editor took me into a cutting room to talk to me about his work, which he loved above all other things. It was an unforgettable day. This man had worked in Hollywood since the 1920s, since the last years of silent film. He had been intimately involved with the whole evolution of montage, of film's inner rhythm—and of narrative flow, which he said was moving faster and faster, as if time were accelerating with the century, as if the cinema, increasingly breathless, were stricken with a mounting and inexplicable sense of urgency.

"It's like planes and cars," he told me. "They have to keep getting faster. Yet our heart and breathing rates haven't changed, nor our digestion. Nor the rhythm of days and nights, of tides, of seasons. Why do films move faster and faster?"

He demonstrated the acceleration of the editing process with films of different vintages. He showed me how in the 1930s you never entered a building without first showing a general view of it (an establishing shot), then a long shot, with if possible a street sign indicating where this was happening, then shots of entrance, stairs, and corridor, before the character reached the person waiting (or not waiting) for him. And he showed me how, over the years, all these once-essential shots had gradually disappeared. He had even been asked by directors or producers to work on old montage jobs, to shorten and tauten them, give them a "modern" look. He had done his best, trying to understand why everyone considered this acceleration inevitable.

He showed me a few sequences, the earliest of them dating from the 1930s, designed to illustrate the meteoric rise to glory of (for instance) a famous singer. Such films typically strung together less than a minute's worth of lively music and linked images: a train's wheels, posters with the star's name in ever bigger letters, presses churning out fat headlines, delirious audiences, bouquets, jewels. "They still haven't improved on it," he told me.

He also showed me silent-movie sequences from which, he believed, it would be impossible to cut a single frame—films he considered eternally perfect, their duration and tempo not subject to the dictates of time, even if these films, for simple technical reasons, might seem hurried and jumpy to us.

He wondered why the soundless images of the past seemed to take shape and fall into place more naturally and with greater rigor and inevitability than talking images, as if the use of speech had introduced a hazier, less polished, less incisive quality into film—perhaps because this newfound facility made it possible to economize on the image, to tell instead of show.

And also because of the prestige and authority of the spoken word.

"An editor shrinks from cutting a character who is talking," he told me. "It's almost bad manners."

He added with a smile, "Particularly if he's a star and has a loud voice."

I saw that man on two or three more occasions. He particularly liked talking to me about time. But he had no theoretical perspective on it. He discussed it like a craftsman for whom the very raw material he shaped, distorted, stretched, and shortened was time itself, the inscrutable and inflexible master he nonetheless managed to mold in his small, dim room.

Gently, lovingly, his hands manipulated the knobs and levers on an editing table.

"No one ever sees this work in a film," he said. "This is the one thing audiences must never see. It's only when it's not done, or badly done, that people notice it."

Among other examples, he spoke of gunfights in Westerns; he spoke from a practical perspective, an experienced perspective. He told me that duels fought to decide which adversary is the quicker trigger (pure Western myth, without the slightest basis in historical reality) are always filmed and edited according to the same invisible model.

The two men (who have waited until the last reel to stage this lethal encounter) walk slowly toward one another, each trying to stare the other down, sometimes exchanging taunts. Cautious bystanders look on. The end is near. We have been expecting this moment for a good hour and a half.

The two men—and we know one of them is living his very last minute—are first shown either together in an establishing shot (showing the two of them against a wide background) or else one after the other; it matters little which. All variations are admissible in this prelude to doom. At the decisive moment, with our nervous systems clamoring for an end to it all, the two men stand stock-still in the dust, hands twitching. Now in real life (supposing such a situation were to arise in real life), things would happen quite differently, for in real life the one who hits or shoots first usually wins. But the cinema plays another kind of game with time and with its old companion, death. I say its old companion because no other medium, not even the battle panoramas of the nineteenth century, has slaughtered such great numbers as the thousands of films we have seen.

Inevitably, the camera first shows the man destined to die. He is the first to grab his gun; he draws and raises the weapon to hip-height. All in one movement.

But he is not the one who wins. At that precise moment the camera switches to the other man, the faster one, the one who is about to kill. He in turn grabs his weapon, raises it, and fires without aiming.

He always hits the target. Depending on the needs of the script, he can simply shoot his opponent's gun from his hand, or wound him (always in the shoulder), or put him down for keeps with a shot through the heart.

With a last grimace, the man who drew first crumples in the dust.

But if the loser's gun was already in position to fire, what on earth was he doing while his opponent was still drawing? He quite simply stood there, six-shooter in hand, for the whole duration of his opponent's shot, not firing, waiting for death. Time has literally been split in two. Apparently in sequence, the two shots in reality describe two actions that took place simultaneously. The trickiest part, the old editor told me, was dragging this fictitious time out to the maximum—we are speaking here of tenths of a second—before our eye, once again caught off guard, can transmit a critical signal to our brains.

Those few instants the designated victim spends waiting for death in this way can seem very brief. But they are not: they are a real fragment of time, time which can be measured and dissected on the editing table. Without coming remotely near the scientists' nanoseconds, which are not only imperceptible but virtually unimaginable fractions of time, editing makes possible a highly refined relationship with time and duration. One second on film is made up of twenty-four frames, and editors tell you that in certain cases one frame, just one frame more or less (that is, one twenty-fourth of a second), can change the rhythm of a scene and almost change the story it tells.

Here, clearly, we are in the realm of the invisible, the imponderable—of what eludes the eye, of what exists but cannot be seen. Here film behaves like a professional conjuror, like a magician who uses his equipment to show us what he wants us to see and nothing else, whose moves slow down only when it suits him, and whose well-schooled hand is quicker than our eye.

Jean-Claude Carrière

* * *

The games film plays with time are so many and so varied that you could write a whole book on this topic alone. Every medium adapts time—that concept which is indefinable yet without which no other concept could exist —to its own needs and permutations. Painting, sculpture, and architecture play the game with a kind of haughty immobility. Every work they generate is a palpable act of defiance, even when it is a painting concerned with only a brief moment of intimacy, with the impression of a train moving swiftly through mist, with a bird soaring in the evening air. Even when it is a canvas claiming to be spontaneous, unbidden, leaping into life without a moment's thought, without preparation. An act of defiance, hurled by one small square of canvas into the face of time, which takes away everything, but which will carry off this one-day wonder of a canvas a little less swiftly than it takes us, than it takes the painter himself. It is the Pyramids' defiance of the sands, the Mayas' of the jungle, Van Gogh's of the revolving sun. So many acts of defiance. Our war against what erases, what shatters and swallows up.

Some paintings, as if eager to marry time, to carve themselves a niche (however small) in time rather than deny it, seem intent on showing the development of an action, on stretching out the duration of a painting, as in the work of Breughel or Poussin, on juxtaposing images which in real life might succeed one another. They arrange perspective and light so that the beholder will read the picture in a specific order. This can be order of importance, order of significance (from surface appear-

110

ance to deeper meaning), or even chronological order ("the action begins at top left...."). By superimposing several hours from the same day (with house windows lamplit but the sky still—or already—bright), René Magritte (among others) often opts to invent a nonexistent time, a jumbled-up time, a time which is his alone and which forever protects the picture from normal aging.

There is also literary time, which comes in various shapes and sizes, with comings and goings, long and short hours, scenes (in Dostoyevsky, for example) with dialogue much too long for the time the author assigns it, with shortcuts, tricks, flashbacks, long introspective pauses, with every imaginable dislocation, for words are nimbler and more cunning than pictures. In some poetic writings we even see time withdraw with a kind of elegance, as if vanquished, paralyzed by an illusion, by an intoxication too heady to resist.

The writers we consider great love to play with time. Here again, perhaps, out of defiance: an attempt to master the ponderousness of writing, of words dragging themselves across the page, lagging far behind thought. (Although sometimes, of course, the opposite occurs, with words soaring into the blue and ideas plodding behind.) In some Shakespeare plays a scene opens, characters appear, meet, talk, act, come and go, receive visitors, and so forth. The scene ends without the principal characters leaving our sight for a second; they have been right there in front of us for ten or fifteen minutes of continuous action, yet we suddenly realize that five years have gone by. Indeed, we generally do not even realize it. We are swept along by the action. We do not have time to think. It takes the stubborn and fastidious vigilance of scholars to catch what they insist is a major error of Shakespeare's (and indeed an obvious chronological impossibility does lurk between the first and second acts of *Othello*). If audiences are swept along unheeding it means that despite the "mistake," or perhaps even because of it, the game Shakespeare plays with time (of which he may or may not have been aware) seems natural to us. Normal chronological logic yields gracefully to the strength and emotional power of a dramatic situation.

If Shakespeare did realize his "mistake," I assume he must at once have swept this down-to-earth objection aside in the interests of higher theatrical imperatives. He probably did not waste two minutes on such clock-watching. He had better things to do. He preferred a streak of lightning to the coziness of settled habit.

In *The Tempest* he even chose to do away with chronology altogether, as if the action proper, which is in truth very simple, were over even before it began, as if Prospero had already decided to forgive his brother. In a state of seeming befuddlement, the castaways stumble ashore on an island ruled by spells. Despite the disaster, their bodies and clothing are unharmed. As if at some foppish court, they exchange absurd puns. They can suddenly fall asleep or wake up, with no night to compel them. They glimpse divinities, vast palaces in the clouds, a nymph, a banquet—all of which will vanish. Two of them move through events in a state of obvious drunkenness, as if to enhance for us the sense of detachment from things, the unreality that stamps the whole play—which ends with the word "free." The island is truly free of space and time. Where are we? When are we? All we can reply is that we are in a theatre.

Here the whole action is internal. We know only that all the characters and Prospero himself will finally have to leave this fleetingly preserved island—just as the audience will have to leave the theatre—and return to the world, there to live more virtuously. The action is clearly situated outside all the usual categories, in a secret, out-of-the-way place, a place each one of us must unendingly seek.

If the inner truth of the action is attained (and it rarely is), all the usual contingencies are forgotten, particularly the everyday treatment of time. Playing with time is a fascinating exercise, and one that should be approached with caution. Peter Brook and I risked it on several occasions, particularly in the *Mahabharata*, for in any case theatrical space (which Peter has called "the empty space") requires a particular time, a time within "main time," which is itself an empty time, ready to accommodate every shift. With it, a whole life can be contained in a gesture. Sometimes the actors themselves did not realize that several time periods were thus fused in the same scene—like Magritte's different degrees of light in one canvas. At such moments you could swear breathing stops and hearts beat backward. A new kind of time worms its fraudulent way into main time which, once again, we are attempting to take by surprise. The author—but with what degree of awareness?—thus expresses a kind of personal defiance, of delight at this display of his technical skill, and also perhaps of his authority, his independence, his freedom.

Jean-Claude Carrière

* * *

In an ordinary novel, in which the rules of time are scru-
pulously respected (the marquise went out at five in the
afternoon, not at any old hour), the game seems simpler
and in a way easier. The author merely has to write
twenty years later or *a childhood scene suddenly came
back to him* for his obliging readers to jump forward or
back, to zigzag, or to indulge an overlong dialogue without noticing that it is too long—in other words, once
again to forget main time, which the clock-watchers say
is unchanging and common to us all, and which in this
case is the time it takes to read.

A very simple, perhaps overly simple, example may
help explain the beginnings of a difference in how literary time and film time are expressed. If in a novel I write
next morning he left his house, I oblige the reader to no
effort. He scarcely notices what I have written. His eyes
and brain, moving so to speak on automatic pilot, retain
only the few elements they need to follow the action
from that phrase: specific, functional elements, dispas-
sionately recorded, without in themselves possessing
emotional force or aesthetic sense, but which would
doubtless be missed if I omitted them. It is a question of
personal appreciation. Everything depends on what
came before and what follows. Every writer can show a
character leaving his house one morning, if that action
seems useful to him. He can also decide not to. It is up
to him.

In any case the phrase is simple, unobtrusive, light.
Even its ordinariness can be forgiven.

In a film it is just as easy to show *a man leaving,* and

114

even a man leaving *his house,* if we already know where he lives. In this case the short filmed scene will be just as easy to grasp as the phrase in the book, just as functional, perhaps just as ordinary.

If we do not know where the character lives, if this is the first time we have seen him leaving, we can have him lock the door with a key, say goodbye to his family or his dog, give a cheerful wave to the neighbors, show he is familiar with the area. All these identification marks stem from the screenplay and staging. The challenge (showing the man leaving *his house*) is simple. What is harder is not to do it too emphatically, too insistently, too heavily, not to waste precious time (in the word's true sense) on it, for time in the movies costs more than elsewhere. The main thing is to conceal the information we dispense behind vital, interesting action.

With a little digging it can be done.

But how do you show in film that it is *next day* and *morning*? If you ask friends this question, you are generally told (after the briefest of intervals for reflection) to use a subtitle. This is not a solution to be rejected out of hand—it has been used and is still used—but it involves calling the written language to the rescue of the visual, as if the latter were infirm. This process is often repugnant to filmmakers, who hold their independence dear. I do not work in film, they say, in order to write on an image what the image itself cannot say. My film is not an illustrated book in reverse. It has its own language, which I owe it to myself to use.

If we refuse to write on the image, or to have a voice-over saying that it is morning, we can always hear a rooster crow (but how do you explain the rooster's presence if the action takes place in the city?), see the sun rising on the horizon (on condition that the day is fine, and then of course it is awfully expensive to shoot very early in the morning), see a garbage truck go past, children trooping to school, a newspaper vendor, what have you. The feel of morning—always supposing it is worth the trouble—can be discreetly and unobtrusively recreated, bothering nobody.

But *next day*? How is that done? By filming a calendar fixed to the wall and a page falling from it? The mother of all clichés. Who would have the gall, unless with satirical intent?

The idea of *next day* is always very difficult to convey, for in film, days and nights do not move in regular sequence as they do in life. They do not even approach such a sequence. There are even *film days*, and *film nights*, which divide time up in a unique way, a way that belongs exclusively to cinema. You can move for example from an *interior—dining-room—day* to an *exterior—battlefield—day*, and so order it that the two scenes following one another in the film similarly follow one another in the supposed reality of the story. Narration time and film time are thus confused. Both scenes take place on the same day.

But while preserving the same cinematic continuity, these two scenes can also take place on two different days in the story. The battlefield scene, just after the dining-room shots, may be next day, next week, next year. Or we may find that the battle had taken place in an earlier year, or even an imaginary year. This battle may be fantasy, dream, a second film within the film.

Given this apparently permanent potential for chaos,

116

only a mysterious inner faculty, intimately linked to our habit of watching films, allows us (most of the time) to reestablish the chronological order desired by the authors. The latter, of course, help us as best they can with changes of lighting and costume, with breaks and resumptions of the musical score (music that continues from one scene to the next tends to unite both in the same continuum). But the essential work is up to us. It is highly likely that an inexperienced viewer, starved of images since birth and suddenly asked to watch one of today's films, would see nothing—even if he understood the language—but a monstrous jumbling of time, just as an extraterrestrial plunked down in a soccer stadium would have absolutely no idea what was going on in the game. Not knowing the rules, having no spectator habits, he would presumably see every game as the same game replayed over and over, whereas we know that from one game to the next there are not two strictly identical seconds to be seen.

As in a game, time sequence in film obeys certain secret rules and even certain tricks, which no one is eager to reveal. Woe to the film that lets audiences see what makes it tick, that meticulously signals and slavishly observes the passage of time. Such laborious servility is instantly apparent, promoting distinct discomfort in spectators even when they are not sure why.

And glory to the film which, while observing the rules, appears to be flouting them.

In the course of the nineteen years Luis Buñuel and I worked together, we dreamed up a respectable middle-class couple whose opinion we regularly invoked. They were the average spectators, a pair of mild French citizens we called Henri and Georgette. At every tricky scene we asked ourselves how they would react. Things invariably reached the point at which Henri, weary of too much boldness, of too much absurd or pointless action, rose and said irritably, "Come on, Georgette, we're leaving, this isn't for us."

In most cases we strove to keep them in the theatre to the bitter end, to think up things they might like, understand, accept, or tolerate despite unexpected behavior or unconventional attitudes on-screen, particularly in transitions from one scene to the next when time and continuity itself were overturned. At every step, during the improvisations that always accompany the writing of a screenplay, Henri would lean over to Georgette (or vice versa) and ask, "Where are we? Is it the same day or the next? Or is it a dream? What do you think, *ma chérie?*"

While it always seemed interesting, and even necessary and healthy, to goad Henri and Georgette, to prod them, to upset them, it seemed equally essential to keep them in the theatre, to avoid pushing them over the edge. Between the two courses the balance was, as always, delicate.

It is the same with the passage of time, that secret bond without which no shared journey is possible. Time is our common baggage, our vehicle, our road. To help us on this journey, to provide useful landmarks, filmmakers use a certain number of processes copied straight from what happens in life: makeup turns hair white, gaits slow down, wrinkles set in as people age. Or else trees have lost their leaves and it is already autumn.

Other techniques seem threatened with extinction,

such as the *dissolve* and the *fade-in,* which ruled the cinema for forty years and which some people, like that Los Angeles editor, recall most fondly. The *fade-in*—a temporary double exposure, of variable duration, of the last frames of one shot and the first frames of the next— always denoted a leap in time, but a short one. The *dissolve*—the gradual disappearance of one image which swims into blackness and disappears completely before another image arises out of that same blackness—invariably signified a longer break.

But as early as the 1920s, adventurous directors were already challenging this formal device. Among them was Luis Buñuel in *Un Chien Andalou,* made in 1928. A character approaches a door and reaches for the handle. In the next shot, which links up with it perfectly, his hand, in closeup, opens the door. Between these two shots, which precisely succeed one another, Buñuel has inserted a fade-in. The two successive images melt into one another in a curious disequilibrium—itself a feat of acrobatics, a flourish, an act of braggadocio—as if to smuggle a mysterious slice of time into an apparent continuity.

Of all these processes, the most common and yet the least obvious is the succession of days and nights.

About fifteen years ago a friend and I were leaving an American Western; something about the way the story was put together bothered us. You might say the film had left us technically discontented. We chatted about it for a while in a café without hitting on the reason for our dissatisfaction. The next day I went back alone to see the film (whose title escapes me) and noticed that two night scenes—campfire scenes in which the cowboys stretch out around the fire, heads on their saddles, while Indians prowl the darkness and villains pull hatbrims down over watchful eyes—were placed much too close to one another in the story. The "film day" that separated them lasted only two or three minutes.

This arrangement, running in the face of nature, broke the overall rhythm of the film at that juncture. From that day on, I was always careful when writing a screenplay to observe a uniform rhythm (as in real life) in the succession of days and nights, to separate film days (which may group several days into one) from film nights (which as a rule are just one night) with more or less equal intervals. Pure cheating, of course, but strangely enough it corresponds to something real, perhaps because we all live with rhythms—cosmic, seasonal, respiratory, cardiac—which we do not even notice.

We know our inner clock suffers if it jumps continents too abruptly; it can also trigger a version of jet lag during a film if its rhythms are not respected. A slight, almost imperceptible discomfort, the result of some unnoticed lapse during the writing of the screenplay and the editing. I mentioned this one day to the Polish director Andrzej Wajda, with whom I was working on *Danton*, and he shouted, "It took me twenty years to find that out!"

Which was about how long it had taken me.

The tempo of a film can be quick or slow. It can also be choppy, staccato, or segmented, if that is what its authors want. But they have to know that the tempo is there, that it is infinitely stronger than we are, and that we would be highly presumptuous to disregard it. You can show just one night in a film (preferably situated around midpoint) or you can show a dozen, but the principle, strangely, is unaltered: out there in the gloom of the movie house we balk at chronological surprises, we prefer a smooth tempo. The ancient terror of eclipses, which seemed to change the course of the stars, lives on in us.

But it is still a mystery—neither Wajda nor I had the answer—why it is so hard to move without a beat from one night to the next in film. Even a brief daylight interlude almost always seems essential to both filmmakers and filmgoers, even during the blackest of *films noirs*. It is as if some fundamental immobility dwells in the heart of the night, a resistance to movement, a sense of time moving at a snail's pace, like the soothing drowsiness we sometimes feel between bouts of sleep. There is a feeling that the stars are not moving, that time itself is resting, that perhaps we are not growing old.

The image of a day between two nights—a street, a hill, a scene in a train—is a trumpet blast, a jangling alarm, a crowing rooster, jolting all our impulses into wakefulness, all the energetic feelings which deep inside us look for sleep when the light fades.

Occasionally, as in Western gunfights, the cinema stretches time out. In thrillers, for example: a dagger plunges toward a throat and—without recourse to slow motion (almost always an aesthetic disaster), once again by a simple editing trick, through a sequence of staggered shots, the dagger never stopping its plunge nor the throat its proffered sacrifice—time drags on and on and sometimes seems to stand still to stimulate our sense of anguished expectation. We catch our breath; time itself hangs motionless.

But generally, and in an equally invisible way, camera and editing speed time up and sometimes even accelerate it. A naked woman starts to dress. She puts on a bra. We leave her to focus on a man who is asking her a question. We return to the woman for her answer, and without any apparent leap in time she is already buttoning her skirt. A second short exchange—a few words from the man, a look from the woman—and she will be almost ready.

Hardly anyone notices this mysterious acceleration. Everything happens as if the woman had dressed *between shots*, in a different temporal continuum from the one we see. The needs of the story as laid out in the screenplay—the female character has to be dressed by the end of the scene—mandate this acrobatic separation, this splitting of time. The question is no longer "What was the gunfighter who drew first doing?" but "What time warp did that woman get dressed in?"

Similarly, skillful and carefully preplanned cutting can show us the consumption of an entire meal in four or five minutes. This is almost always the case. Meals are invariably very brief in film, even when they are the subject of the film, as in *Babette's Feast*.

Taking a first nibble at her *hors d'oeuvre* or a first spoonful of soup, the mistress of the house asks a question. At this point we move to one of the guests, who is already emptying his own soup plate as he answers her. A second guest now joins the conversation (here again without any obvious leap in time, so that the conversation appears to be unfolding normally) while already helping himself to a piece of lobster. Now the mistress of the house (with her own lobster almost polished off) speaks up again—which of course means another change of shot—and then we are given a silent shot of the aged aunt looking at the other diners as she helps herself to leg of mutton. Another guest makes a remark as he polishes of the last bits of that same leg of mutton, and then yet another guest—in another shot—moves on to the next item on the menu. And so it goes. Very soon we are ready for cheese and coffee.

Cloaked by the dialogue, the meal races by at top speed. If the cutting is good, as it was in *Babette's Feast* (where the director's problems were made even more difficult by the very fact that the meal was the subject of the film, so that we all kept our eyes on it), and if dialogue or action is interesting enough to monopolize our attention, we do not notice this anomaly. Physical action, everyday action, whose tempo and duration are perfectly familiar, yields to dramatic action. It gives way. Fiction has wiped out reality, and once again we accept its victory.

Many editors have wondered, and still wonder, about these small technical mysteries, about the transactions that occur at each change of shot between action, dialogue, eye, and brain, not to mention our subconscious, which doubtless shrinks at the idea of following a long scene (such as a quickly boring meal) in real time. Here again we are at the innermost sanctum of cinematic narrative and form, at the point where nothing more can be said, unless we launch into a philosophical and (why not?) metaphysical discussion—which would of course explain nothing.

All we are seeing—or, thanks to editing, not seeing —is a multitude of tiny subterfuges in the midst of what appears to be reality, subterfuges which add up to make a new kind of temporal continuity. Action moves faster than film. Events, acts, words hide out between frames. Eating or dressing scenes are obvious examples, as are scenes of mountain climbing or swimming across rivers, or the progress of a battle between two armies. But there are other, subtler examples: a plane ride (sometimes just a few seconds), climbing stairs, an emotion appearing on a face, decision making, emotional metamorphosis. How many times have we seen a man seize a woman in his arms; she struggles, resists, screams, even hits him—and then suddenly yields, is still? Her arms enfold the shoulders of the man holding her, and soon their lips meet. The supreme cliché; we have all smiled at it. But if we care to look closely we may instead recognize it for the remarkable contraction it is: a sequence of events (which in real life would have kept this man and woman busy for weeks, even months) squeezed into less than half a minute.

We are thus caught between the absurd and the boring, between the necessary but excessive simplification of an action and a more faithful, and consequently more elaborate, imitation of what we call (and have always called) reality.

In the very heart of an action, of a scene, the increasing tendency in cinema is to cut, often and boldly, to leap directly from one phase in a scene to a later phase, still in the same physical setting and with the same characters. The old need to narrate a scene continuously, from start to finish, has withered away. Instead of adhering to what in the 1960s they called "real time" (although no one ever knew what that meant, since no action on film—itself a time-within-a-time—can possibly be measured against reality), contemporary cinema seems ever more dislocated, readier to skip from high point to high point, without concerning itself too much with the logical continuity of a scene. The editing techniques that astounded us thirty years ago in Jean-Luc Godard's *Breathless* (there was a long scene with two people in a bedroom where he selected only those moments that interested him, and simply juxtaposed them) we now routinely expect to see in the majority of films. The new language had been mastered relatively quickly both by those who practiced it and those who watched it.

Editing and special effects are what currently dominate filmmaking. This is of course the basic video style we already mentioned: a dizzy proliferation of shots, and jerky action that looks like the product of channel-hopping. They seem designed to stop us from thinking or understanding or even seeing, for fear perhaps of revealing an immense void. In any case, this fashion indicates that people are still intoxicated by technology. Who knows whether this is a sign of youth or of premature senility? In some films it is the contrary phenomenon that comes close to astonishing us—the survival of traditional montage, the no-longer-needed walks down long corridors. As for the moments of reflection, the hesitations, when once upon a time (in the films of, say,

Michelangelo Antonioni or Theodoros Angelopoulos) we could follow every one of a character's impulses or ponder every possible bifurcation of action or feeling, they are increasingly withheld. I often go back to the last sequence in Stanley Kubrick's *2001: A Space Odyssey*, one of film's most beautiful flirtations with time. It takes place in a kind of four-star intergalactic hotel. Time itself seems to be the main character, aging before our eyes; wordlessly, without explanation, without any other event to mar its dissolution. We are free to wander at will: a true mystery. But all too often, through a tempo insistent to the point of oppressiveness, we have one vision, just one, forced upon us, and our chances of entering the scene ourselves, of bringing to it some of our own feelings or ideas, are increasingly threatened, diminished, rebuffed.

They are killing time. In film as elsewhere.

I sometimes wonder whether this more or less deliberate destruction of time is not one of cinema's secret obsessions: to eliminate time physically, obliterate it, to build an illusion so powerful that audiences truly cease to age and leave the cinema rejuvenated—or at least feeling rejuvenated.

Doubtless this applies to the flashback, that wonderfully cinematic narrative technique much in fashion in the 1940s. It first shows us something, happy or sad, happening in the present, then yanks us back into the past to seek the origins of the present action—as if we were paddling back upstream on some causal waterway—before bringing us back once more for the end of the story the film is telling. Time is thus truly denied. You can indeed go back. Contrary to what the philosophers say, the same water does flow twice. An hour and a half later we find ourselves at our point of departure, which is now our destination. A loop of time closes, time which has been virtually preserved, as if immune from ordinary aging. When we come out onto the sidewalk at the end of the afternoon, we are surprised to see night at hand and the streetlights lit.

And then, at a single leap, we age. We catch up with past, or lost, time. The illusion is rent asunder. It was all a mistake. Someone has had the gall to play with us, make us believe in the impossible—with our permission of course, with our help even. When Jean Gabin kills himself in the first scene of *Le Jour se lève,* we know that this is not the end of his story. They did not hire a big star to have him vanish in the first few minutes. We will certainly see him again, alive and kicking.

But we will no longer see him in the same way, since we know he is walking toward death.

Thus the problem of time, or rather of cinematic duration, which might have seemed merely technical or aesthetic, almost inevitably ties in with other aspects of the complex, indefinable relationship a filmmaker maintains with his audience (of which he too is a member). Playing with time, whether you speed it up, slow it down, cut and splice it, dissect it, or even forget it, is an organic component of the language of film, a part of the vocabulary, the syntax.

Nothing in this constant and constantly renewed relationship is innocent. Nothing, not even naiveté, and still less clumsiness. More or less wakeful, more or less dulled, we forge second by second an intimate, diverse, sometimes contradictory contact with film. And time is the most important component of this contact. But it remains unseen, like the wind shaking the trees.

Since its beginnings, film has taken an almost sensual pleasure in reconstructing the past, often with such extreme care that you could be fooled—as long as the camera remains unobtrusive. For even a hint of technical or optical bravura in a scene set in the Middle Ages at once alerts us to the filmmaker's presence, to the presence of complex equipment, and the spell is broken. The dream of innocence remains elusive: we have seen too many films and films about films and about the making of films for some knowledge not to have stuck. Even with the Knights of the Round Table or Jason and his Argonauts, if the panoramic shot is too clever or the zoom effect is too labored, we at once sense the presence of a full-scale team complete with floodlights and sound equipment. An anachronism unseen but felt by everyone to a degree that depends on the state of his knowledge.

Details no one else had previously noticed can make nonsense of historical scenes. During the first screenings of *The Return of Martin Guerre,* which takes place in a village in sixteenth-century southern France, we invited the people of the region to view the film. Among them was an old mountain herdsman who said it was his first visit to the cinema, which seemed highly likely.

One thing worried him after the showing. He told us about it. "When the villagers go to Toulouse," he said, "the cows there are Friesians. There weren't any in these parts at that time."

An insurmountable objection; and one, sure enough, that justified his rejection of the whole film.

But I do not believe I have seen anything of this kind to compare with an American film of the 1950s, *The Prodigal Son*, with Lana Turner and Edmund Purdom. Vaguely biblical, this film showed among other things the ancient custom of the harlots' wall, on which a man would inscribe the sum he was willing to pay for a certain woman.

So Edmund Purdom, burning with love for Lana Turner, approaches the wall, armed with hammer and chisel, and begins to write. Naturally, so as to waste no time, skillful cutting showed us the whole message almost at once and—in a masterly compromise between producers and historical advisers—in cuneiform script and in English we saw A PIECE OF SILVER FOR TAMARA.

They could have opted not to show the inscription, or found some other gimmick, or cut the scene. But film is so besotted with the past that it has never balked at toothsome incongruities of this kind. Remember Faulkner's laughter!

It is impossible to name a period of the past that has failed to spark the cinema's interest. Nothing eludes its investigation of time gone by—not prehistory, nor the Dark Ages, nor myth and legend. (It is just as curious about its own past, now a century old. It is already returning to its own childhood and youth, with a kind of joyful nostalgia, even dwelling lovingly on its fumblings and its mistakes.) The past is its territory. It resurrects the past. It invents materials, fabrics, arms, gestures, costumes, languages. It brings Vikings into the heart of Africa and takes Martians to Babylon. Maciste, musclebound hero of Italian "mythological" spectaculars, meets and fights Hercules. Where exactly? And when? Very hard to say. In any case the film throws in a cruel sultan, tortured slaves, garish rebels, a glamorous woman (scantily clad and given to wearing tiaras), shaggy monsters, battlements, orgies, white horses, and on occasion even firearms: a grand summing-up of our history.

In these extraordinary journeys, which go from remotest prehistory to future ages, the game with time may sometimes look naive, overdone, extraordinarily clumsy. Historical fiction—telling the past as it might have been —is one of the hardest forms to bring off, for we look upon history as a series of real and undisputed events. Any questioning of what we think we know of our past runs smack into our disbelief. It can also rub national pride the wrong way: the past is often holy ground, plowed once and for all. No sowing of weeds, please, or even of unfamiliar seeds.

Yet beyond naiveté, error, or sacrilege, this irresistible game with time gone by imparts a very special flavor to our experience as spectators. A new dimension—fashion—intrudes upon our relationship with the image.

That a given fashion can transform the past has long been known, ever since the Romantics, for example, saw and portrayed the Gothic period in their own way—somber, skeletal, always nocturnal—even going so far as to alter old monuments, as Viollet-le-Duc did with his modifications to the roof of Notre-Dame in Paris.

In film the process is even more obvious. Every stage in the life of film has imposed its own fashion on the historical era it depicts. These fashions come and go quickly. The ancient Rome of the 1920s is not at all the same as the technicolor Rome of the 1950s. The present changes the past, in film as elsewhere, but in film it changes the past at great speed. We adapt that past, usually without even realizing it, to our taste, our habits, our way of seeing, so much so that in the 1950s we considered the ancient Rome of the 1920s old hat; and 1950s Rome, in turn, looks absurd and unwatchable to us now.

And it gets more complicated.

If today I view a René Clair silent film, *An Italian Straw Hat,* inspired by a Labiche play of the nineteenth century, I see a turn-of-the-century film, a film that looks to me as if it was shot around 1900. Yet in fact the film was made in 1928, and to make it, René Clair undertook a thorough historical reconstruction, creating settings, finding costumes, marshaling a fleet of hansom cabs— labor that today escapes our notice. When we see the film today, the twenty-five years between the filming and the period the film depicts have mysteriously vanished. *An Italian Straw Hat* has turned into a turn-of-the-century film. The two periods have become confused. Or perhaps we should say the three periods, to take into account the period in which the original play first saw the light of day.

And it is easy to see that in the future this blurring of eras will intensify. Already, in a silent film of the 1920s (an Italian or American "epic" set in the ancient or Islamic world, such as *Ben Hur, Scipio the African, The Thief of Baghdad*), every component—grainy texture, black-and-white photography, silence, the jerky gait of the characters (an instant sign of the past)—everything

131

seems to contribute to a strange synthesis, everything seems to thrust the films into ever remoter pasts, until finally they seem to have gone all the way back to the very period they recreate.

If we possessed newsreels of those periods, shot by cameramen accompanying the real Roman armies into Africa, how would they differ from the images served up in *Scipio the African*?

Because of our mental laziness, our fascination with the past and our propensity for daydreaming, abetted by the rapid aging of technology, sequences from *Scipio the African* showing elephants at the battle of Zama and war chariots attacking into a sandstorm have started to look like sequences from a film shot in ancient Rome long before the invention of film. There are times when I am ready to swallow the whole thing, even the exaggerated makeup and theatrical acting. Knowing that all these feverishly busy characters are already dead, that the actors and extras in the film (except for a handful of hundred-year-olds) have already gone off to that vast domain where the older dead await them, I could easily believe that it was the real Scipio standing there, giving his historic commands—just as I can see the real General Rommel, also in black and white, directing German troops on the same African soil in the Second World War.

The deserts of the American West have been the setting for many biblical films. Moses and Solomon have crossed California. Napoleon has been forced to retreat from Moscow across Canada's snows. The African forest, with or without Tarzan, has often journeyed to Costa Rica or

Mexico. Popocatepetl has occasionally stood in for Mount Fuji, while cowboys and Indians have clashed in the bare hills of southern Spain.

Besides playing with time, cinema has also turned geography upside down. It has costumed the planet in every conceivable disguise. On several occasions scenes set in Normandy have been filmed in South Africa among similar meadows and similar cows. In Paris there is a street—just one—where London scenes can be shot. The houses on it, or at least down one side of it, are built in the English style. I have also seen a whole London neighborhood built in Mexico City; Moscow in Berlin; Paris in Lisbon. In his adaptation of Kipling's *The Man Who Would Be King,* John Huston reconstructed India and Afghanistan in Morocco, and filmed the Himalayas in the Alps. Conversely, it was in Afghanistan that Peter Brook made *Meetings with Remarkable Men.* He even had *trompe-l'oeil* pyramids built there.

There are no limits to this landscape-swapping. It is generally resorted to for reasons of convenience and economy, but some directors seem to delight in such gymnastics for their own sake, with the illusion of space an extension of the manipulation of time. It would take endless digging to distinguish what is real from what is not real in a film. But why bother? In any case, the planet we recognize on the screen is not ours.

The cinema is a magic box in which transported space and jumbled eras, shaken up together as if in a raffle drum, finally mingle as a kind of single time past. This of course presupposes the participation of our eye and all our other senses. But well before the approach of the millennium, we had been insisting that nothing outside us exists with any certainty, that no image is real unless we have decided it is.

I already have that feeling today. By tomorrow it will no doubt be sharper, stronger. Let us leap a thousand years ahead—an exercise cinema has made almost familiar. The time separating the film *Scipio the African* from the ancient world will become relative, shrinking constantly until one day it will utterly disappear, just as it has done in *An Italian Straw Hat.*

We already have historical examples of the phenomenon: the dark centuries in particular, those of the early Middle Ages, have shrunk. Some centuries are markedly shorter than others. And we confuse them with their neighbors. We readily mistake a fourteenth-century book of hours for a picture of Carolingian society. We speak of a "pre-Columbian object" without specifying its date (a vague zone several millennia long) and even of a "pre-historic tool" (several score millennia). Our sense of time is so relative, so tied to the average duration of our personal passage on the planet, that we are profoundly incapable of imagining a very long duration, of the kind which paleontologists, for example, ascribe to the evolution of species.

Millions of years: these words mean nothing to us. They are just words. We cannot begin to imagine what they convey. That is why, as time flows relentlessly on, we will one day have Greco-Roman films and Assyrian or pre-Columbian films. Every period, whether it occurred before or after the actual invention of cinema, will tend to blur into other periods (except to scholars, who will probably be few and far between, isolated, perhaps ill-treated). And in the collective mind, which through laziness and lack of imagination differentiates very little between things, Mark Antony will have Marlon Brando's features, followed by the surprise of seeing another film with the same features given to Napoleon, so that some will marvel at the resemblance between the two great men.

For this to happen two conditions are necessary. First, that people go on watching Marlon Brando's films. There is no guarantee of this. And second, that no other great actor of the future create equally admired portraits of Mark Antony and Napoleon, thus supplanting Brando's performances, or bizarrely coexisting with them.

But overriding both conditions is, of course, the assumption that people in the future will go on watching films. Here again, no guarantees. Moving and talking pictures will certainly assume different forms. They are already doing so: screens get wider, sound systems change. Soon holographic theatre troupes will visit our homes to put on the show of our choice; so will ballet companies and wild-animal shows, and there will be synthetically imaged naked dancers tolerant of our caresses. It is almost certain, however regrettable it may seem, that our techniques will age precisely because they are techniques, that our color and even our Cinemascope films will one day seem as downright obsolete as yesterday's black-and-white films now (alas) seem outdated to some.

This threat of imminent demise has hung over cinema since the very beginning. When the Lumière Brothers opened the first public cinema at the Grand Café on the Paris boulevards on December 28, 1895, they thought that their attraction would last through the holiday period, and perhaps even for a few years more, but that people would quickly tire of it, the way you tire of a toy. At its birth cinema already felt temporary. Or, to be precise, film projected in an auditorium did.

We still feel that threat. Talk of crisis is always in the air. Cinemas are closing, done in by disaffection and speculation. Of course we see more and more films, but we see them on television, or on cassettes. The American market is still holding up—but for how much longer?

That is what they say, anyway. Is it true or false? Every prophet has moments of weakness. For cinema the millennium is always at hand. The end is always near.

What will be left?

It can be argued that we filmmakers will no longer interest anyone in the future but a handful of nostalgia enthusiasts. They are already colorizing some of our black-and-white masterpieces, *Citizen Kane* for example, with the pathetic commercial aim of fobbing them off in their electronic makeup as recent works. (The pitfalls of "newness" have been around a long time: when will we see Goya's engravings in color?) In the same vein, they can be expected, unless we are vigilant, to remodel, reedit, enhance, and similarly adulterate all our old films.

Unless I am wrong. Which is entirely possible. We are so often mistaken when we discuss what has not yet happened. Besides, when it concerns form, all speculation on the future is profoundly futile. Just as planting a tree is an act without price, just as it is vital to fight the good fight against those destroying the Earth and leaving nothing for tomorrow, so it strikes me as irrelevant to wonder what tomorrow's films will be, what today's films will be in the future. Nothing is so unpredictable as the future. We do not make films today for twenty-first-century viewers any more than we put Shakespeare on for fifteenth-century spectators. Every form of expression is contemporary. We work for those who share this moment of history with us. Here and now.

Tomorrow and elsewhere: what can we say about it?

Time, the sense of time, the very idea of time's flow, of the possibility of change, of the existence of a past piling up behind us, of a future opening up ahead—it is all too recent an invention. We are not yet used to time, we have not tamed it, not by a long chalk. Fourteenth-century peasants, who saw Christ as having lived (more or less) in their great-grandfather's lifetime, had tamed it better than we have. In a world that scarcely changed, yesterday was still within touching distance. Tomorrow remained similar to today, with no hope of a single new image—except, at certain periods, for Judgment Day.

At the beginning of the sixteenth century, abandoning the ancient tradition of depicting the past with the architecture and costumes of the present, they began to paint Caiaphas, in gospel illustrations, wearing Jewish garb and high priest's headgear. So too for the Jews, the Roman soldiers, and soon also for the knights of the

Middle Ages. They were the first serious attempts at reconstruction, at historical realism. At first, time tiptoed shyly in, but it soon waxed bolder.

In the same period—for the past is never unaccompanied by the future—Thomas More published his *Utopia,* soon to be followed by a host of imaginative works about a world to come, for better or worse: in any case a different future, one we could dream of. Time had now split apart to move both forward and back, and century by century the fissure widened. Today it is vast. People readily talk of the Big Bang—fifteen billion years ago already—and of the almost certain extinction (oh, the pity of it!) of the galaxies. "Our little life," as Shakespeare called it, still rounded with the same sleep, has now extended its dreams to the very brink of the infinite.

But while descriptions of future worlds invariably stimulate the imagination, nothing ages so fast as the future, for the present is hot on its heels. The "errors" of anticipation are many and have been pointed out many times. Countless authors have blown the world to smithereens in order to play in the rubble, but few of them, even in the twentieth century, ever dared predict the demographic and ecological catastrophe which is ours. And we would look in vain through novels from the 1930s and even the 1940s for references to plastics, water shortages, desertification. The future generally remains tailored to our immediate dimensions; we inflate our petty problems to fit vast spaces.

So science fiction ages even faster in films than in books, for it has to give visible shape and substance to the future. It has to invent fashions for the future—a hopeless undertaking, since fashion lives only today.

And time and the depiction of time, like the depiction of space, are subject to fashion. As we approach the millennium we can look back on how the visionaries of the 1920s and 1930s imagined us. And if some of those visions still dazzle us (Fritz Lang's *Metropolis*, for instance, or Chaplin's *Modern Times*), others look terribly sketchy, or mannered, or wrong. That future already belongs to the past, a past which today speaks to us only of the past.

So however we imagine the future, whatever shapes and colors we lend it, the pictures we create grow old. And just as we cannot recognize the period we live in from the silent black-and-white predictions of the 1920s, in the same way all our images of today will tomorrow be images of yesterday.

What is probable is that tomorrow, like today, the past will quite simply expand. A constant stream of new films will swell the number we already possess, creating a situation so complex that all attempts at simplification will necessarily be welcome.

Simplification and selection. And selection's chief weapon is oblivion, time's old companion and ruthless henchman.

A friend and I one day made a tally of the eight thousand stage plays performed in Paris in the nineteenth century. At a generous estimate, only forty or so are still produced in France. They include a handful of "classics," *The Lady of the Camellias, Cyrano de Bergerac, Ubu Roi,* a few Hugos and Mussets and—the most frequently performed of all—a dozen comedies by Labiche. Plus foreign plays from Goethe to Ibsen. Let us say, to be generous, eighty plays from all quarters.

One out of a hundred. Not even one for each year of the century.

At this brief remove of a hundred years, it is a grim casualty rate. I imagine it is much the same for other European countries. The attrition rate would be comparable, in fact probably worse, if we tallied the soap-opera-style literature the Romantic Age gobbled so greedily. Almost nothing is left of it. And everything suggests that the same fate awaits us.

Admittedly, the nineteenth century did not have television to extend the life of dramatic works, to keep mediocrity determinedly alive. Yet even with our new audience-reaching techniques, it is almost impossible to imagine that the popular American TV series of the 1960s and 1970s, the exact equivalent of the last century's melodramas, will still be watched fifty years from now.

As for the films we admire and love, films we cannot imagine vanishing from memory, they too will be covered over by oblivion, devoured, lost, destroyed. Already, many of yesterday's masterpieces are never seen —unless we ask for them at film libraries. Many have vanished or have been mutilated. From time to time in the years ahead we will be offered "a film our grandparents loved" as an object of curiosity.

And sometimes they will be remade to fit the fashion of the day. All that is already being done.

In any case, it's of little importance. We don't work for the future, for poor overworked posterity whose tastes are a closed book to us. We work simply for oblivion. Like Paul Hervieu and Georges de Portoriche, authors illustrious a hundred years ago, we too will be expunged. Other names will take our place, to be erased in their turn.

We are all aware, too, that oblivion strikes more quickly all the time. Films which misfire on opening night, which are overtaken by events, by the success of other films, by a wave of sour critical reaction or any other kind of rejection phenomenon—such unfortunates are strangled at birth, and almost never get a second chance. In film it is now or never.

Another indicator: time moves forward fast, faster than it used to. That Los Angeles film editor felt it. No one can tell us why.

Conversely, the image-as-record, the image-as-archive, the image-as-history, long despised, now looks as if it will last longer. History is going to need us. With the inauguration in 1988 of the Paris Vidéothèque, the very first video library, we have entered an era of accessible and proliferating archives. Every country, region, institution, and big corporation will create its own audio-visual archives. The movement is already well under way, even fashionable, and the appearance of durable numerical aids will further its development. In a few years, tomorrow, it will obviously be very difficult to teach the history of the twentieth century without recourse to cinema and television images.

The whole century has been filmed, by amateurs, journalists, war correspondents, spies. Political addresses, invasions, refugee flows, expeditions to far countries, fights-of-the-century, famous writers' remarks —it has all been recorded and more or less well preserved. A broad and confused memory with ill-defined frontiers is here and there dismembered and lost. It is a monster memory, which already poses vast problems of adjustment, utilization, and above all interpretation. An intrusive and probably necessary memory. Everything suggests that eras to come will poke through our debris and bitterly regret our carelessness, just as we already regret that no one filmed or recorded Marcel Proust or Franz Kafka. Although, when you think about it a little, what sort of curiosity would that have satisfied? Media hunger? Literary voyeurism? Are we really sure that our contact with the works would have been improved?

Thus, having witnessed certain moments of history, the filmed image will itself enter history. Having seen the light of day in a century that has told the story of all the centuries, it will become history's instrument and an object of investigation.

When producers of certain TV programs use sequences from feature films, performed by actors, to illustrate historical events, as if those scenes were contemporary documents, viewers are told it is a film, a simulation. But our natural visual and mental indolence soon overlooks such warnings, which are in any case unobtrusive. Once again, we allow ourselves to be seduced and blinded by the image.

And the collective memory has the same shortcomings as our own: it schematizes, it confuses, it distorts, it forgets. Just as we award ourselves the glory role in certain episodes of our life, finally believing in our own lies, so whole peoples lie to themselves. They invent for themselves nonexistent virtues and heroic behavior. They wipe away shameful episodes; they never instigate disasters or wars. They celebrate illusory victories. Even in the official history textbooks they let the historians cheat. All peoples behave in this fashion, innocently and knowingly. Concerning the battle of Poitiers—the famous eighth-century Frankish victory over the Arabs, a centuries-old bedrock of France's sense of national superiority and contempt for other races—a Sorbonne professor once confidentially told me: "We know now that the battle of Poitiers didn't happen. And if it did happen, it didn't happen at Poitiers. And if it happened somewhere other than Poitiers, we lost it."

If this is the case with historical truth, why shut the door on fiction on the grounds that it would be necessarily and irredeemably false?

Would-be reality and so-called fiction are moving ever closer. And the phenomenon is not confined to cinema. It has entered the mainstream of contemporary historical research. In our ambiguous (and by definition, impossible) attempt to make the past live again, or at least to understand and restore it, the imaginary has become as important an instrument as the actual event. Reality no longer suffices for the writing of history. Facts are dry and incomplete. We want to know what our predecessors thought, the stuff of their desires, fantasies, and dreams. So film, which strives to recreate not only the forms but also the mindsets of the past (mindsets that are, of course, unverifiable), has pride of place in this new mosaic.

It is not only our past. It is also our way of looking at the past. *Scipio the African* can already be seen as a newsreel about ancient Rome, but it can also instruct us about the beginnings of Fascist Italy, about the Duce's fanatical dreams, about his secret designs on North Africa, a land ripe for conquest.

And so it goes; film enters history through all doors. It remakes history, it helps recount the past, it becomes history itself. Fellini's *Satyricon* can be seen as a vision showing us some distant planet, but if you look carefully, you will also see a film that is unmistakably about the year 1968.

Besides, the future will mix everything up. The order it imposes on the history books will be its own, and we cannot guess what that will be. Authentic places or manufactured sets, real streets or studio mockups—in three or four hundred years, who will know the difference? Eric von Stroheim rebuilt his Tyrol, his castles, and his Vienna in Hollywood, a whole precise world he bore within himself, transformed, redesigned, perhaps more real than the real one. Hitchcock did the same with the deceptively placid setting of the English stately home. Perhaps one day their pretend films, their filmed simulations, will be the only reality left of an age doomed to oblivion.

Perhaps one day *Joan the Woman,* filmed in 1916 by Cecil B. de Mille on American soil, a continent of whose existence Joan of Arc never dreamed, will be analyzed as a historical document on the life and death of France's Maid.

Perhaps *Sommersby,* an adaptation of *The Return of Martin Guerre,* itself an adaptation of a true story, will one day be seen as a film set in a small sixteenth-century village in southern France whose peasants grow tobacco with the help of black slaves at the end of a long civil war.

On the other hand, some films which we now prize for the story they tell—crime, adventure, romance—or for their emotional power, for the quality of their acting, may in a few centuries be regarded as straight documentaries, background reports on cities or landscapes. Perhaps the struggles waged in Elia Kazan's *On the Waterfront* will interest nobody, and even Marlon Brando's name will be forgotten. However, a handful of students of New York history or of twentieth-century social movements may continue to pick over the film from the sociological point of view.

As Eric Rohmer once wrote, "A good film is *also* a documentary."

If we had been able to preserve filmed records, archives, moving images, or sounds from certain eighteenth- or nineteenth-century entertainments long since consigned to oblivion, we might occasionally turn to them nowadays with interest, with the slightly morbid curiosity we bring to the parades of flickering ghosts marching past us in old newsreels.

It would be as good a form of survival as any other. Like a second shot at an afterlife. What we say may one day seem boring, childish, or old hat, but we ourselves will perhaps survive. Perhaps the "documentaries" we unwittingly produce will one day be fought over by small specialized groups of students.

But it's all speculation. Indeed, at the first mention of the passage of time, speculation and digression (which time itself kindles and sweeps away) take over. Like every other human activity, cinema is inextricably locked into time. We occasionally try to rest by the roadside, even to take a few steps to left or right or to the rear. In vain. Impossible to stem the flow. We are like the ant in the African proverb, swept away in the rushing waters of a storm drain. "Very well," he says, "I will follow you, but only because you are the police!"

At least the cinema amuses, at least the cinema offers the balm of oblivion, time's inseparable brother, to both creator and audience. Like every art form, the cinema plays a cunning hand against the great master. It marks the cards, it bluffs. The halt it proposes is illusory, like every halt, but it can be refreshing. It can also be rousing and stimulating, for it forces us to wakefulness (in the best of cases; in the others, oblivion is enough). As Heinrich Böll wrote, "Reality demands our active, not passive, attention." We could say exactly the same about fiction. Active attention—in the very best of cases. Otherwise, we must be satisfied with boredom and unsung toil.

Basically a technical process, even a merely mechanical one, cinema has nevertheless explored the most delicate areas, the subtlest shades of feeling. Originally a fairground attraction, it has nevertheless invented and perfected a new and extraordinarily complex language. Conceived for the purpose of depicting "reality," it nevertheless maintains the strangest and most contradictory relations with that same reality. Imprisoned (like all things) within time, it nevertheless struggles to break free of time. (And failing that, it uses its wits.) Finally, born to the impermanence of the peepshow, it nevertheless struggles to endure, exorcising itself as best it can every step of the way.

146

THE VANISHING SCREENPLAY

You will occasionally hear an actor say, "I'm going to do this film. The screenplay isn't fabulous, but my part's good." I, who live by writing screenplays, have never quite understood what this means. I am equally puzzled when friends who want to please me say, "I really liked your screenplay. The dialogue was wonderful, although the film wasn't all that good."

I fail to see how you can dissociate a screenplay from a film, appreciate them separately. I personally cannot do it with other people's films. I can admire a cameraman's framing, or be embarrassed by an actor's performance, but I either like or dislike a film as a whole. I have no real idea what kind of beast a *well-directed* but *badly written* film might be. It would be a hybrid, almost unimaginable creature. A film is always a thing in itself, a more or less successfully executed whole, with disappointing or exciting parts. Inventive, passionate direction can sometimes breathe life into a commonplace little story. That happens. Conversely, a mediocre or arrogant director can hideously sabotage a good story. That happens too, alas. But in that case the original screenplay has disappeared, the victim of foul play; it no longer exists. So how can we still say it's good?

In fact, a good screenplay is one that gives birth to a good film. Once the film exists, the screenplay is no more. It is probably the least visible component of the finished work. It is the first incarnation of a film and appears to be a self-contained whole. But it is fated to undergo metamorphosis, to disappear, to melt into another form, the final form.

I was twenty-five and had just published a first novel when my publisher, Robert Laffont, knowing I was interested in film, suggested that I enter a curious contest. He had just signed a contract with Jacques Tati to publish two books based on Tati's films, *Monsieur Hulot's Holiday* and *My Uncle* (the latter being then in the throes of shooting). Tati had suggested that Laffont ask several of his younger authors to write one chapter each of *Monsieur Hulot's Holiday*. After which Tati himself would choose the storyteller.

I agreed, and won—thus deciding, although I didn't yet know it, the course of my life. Jacques Tati chose my chapter, which I had written in the first person, speaking through the mouth of one of the film's characters, a dapper old gent who continually strolls the town with his wife, his hands folded behind his back, spending three or four boring weeks each year this way: a man whose holiday is about to be turned upside-down by Monsieur Hulot.

Tati suggested we meet in his office off the Champs-Elysées. I entered with pounding heart. For the very first time in my life I was in a production company's premises. This man whom I admired so much ushered me in. He spoke little, but the gaze he directed at me was piercing. First he asked what I knew about film. I said I loved it more than anything in the world, that I went to the Cinémathèque three times a week, that I . . .

He raised a hand.

"No, what I mean is, what exactly do you know about films? About how films are made?"

I answered truthfully that I knew almost nothing.

"You have never worked in films?"

"No, sir."

He at once called his editor, Suzanne Baron (with whom I would later work on several films, including Volker Schlöndorff's *The Tin Drum*), and said to her, "Suzanne, take this young man and show him what film is."

With unerring instinct, in the space of three or four minutes, Tati had just given me my first great lesson: to handle film, from whatever angle—even if it is only to write a book based on a film—you must know how films are made; you must know, and preferably master, the techniques of film. You cannot assume, with literary aloofness, that you have no need to know about this hodgepodge of specialized equipment and cottage-industry skills.

On the contrary. You must master these skills, live with them, grapple with them.

That same day Suzanne Baron took me into an editing room in the building and sat me down in front of a mysterious machine called a Moviola. She took the first reel of *Monsieur Hulot's Holiday* and fitted it into the machine. She switched on a bulb somewhere. Pictures began appearing on the tiny screen in front of me. Then, by manipulating a metal lever, Suzanne showed me how you could move the film forward, backward, stop it on a single frame, speed it up or slow it down. A little magic lever, and my first game with time.

When the equipment was in place, Suzanne put a screenplay of the movie on the table beside me, and uttered a simple, unforgettable phrase, which was my second big lesson of the day.

She put one hand on the screenplay, the other on the reel of film, and said, "The whole problem is to go from this to this."

The whole problem. You could take those words as a rather commonplace remark, but in fact they contain the whole huge secret of the transition. They clearly state the essential: that making a film is truly a work of alchemy, of transmuting paper into film. Transmutation. Transforming matter itself.

Everyone knows that when shooting is over, screenplays generally end up in studio wastebaskets. They are discarded, quickly done away with; they have turned into something else; they no longer have any kind of existence. I have often compared this metamorphosis to the caterpillar's transformation into a butterfly. The caterpillar's body already contains all the cells and all the colors of the butterfly. It is the *potential* butterfly. But it cannot fly. Yet the urge to fly is deeply buried in its most secret essence.

The screenplay is not the last stage of a literary journey. It is the first stage of a film. Jacques Tati and Suzanne Baron taught me that in a matter of minutes thirty-five years ago, and each day's experience confirms it. A screenwriter has to be much more a filmmaker than a novelist. Of course knowing how to write does no harm, but writing for film is a specific and quite difficult exercise that resembles no other. The screenwriter must bear in mind at all times, and with almost obsessive insistence, that what he is writing is fated to disappear, that a necessary metamorphosis awaits it.

Of all writing, a screenplay is the one doomed to the smallest readership: at most, a hundred people. And each of those readers will consult it for his own particular, professional ends. Actors will often see in it only their own part (what is known as the "selfish reading"). Producers and distributors will look only for signs of its potential success. The production manager will count the number of extras, of night shoots. The sound engineer will be hearing the film as he turns the pages, while the head cameraman will be seeing the lighting, and so on. A whole series of special readings. It is an instrument, which is read, annotated, dissected—and discarded. I am well aware that some collectors keep them, and that sometimes they are even published, but that's only if the film works. Then they live on in its slipstream.

Writing for film seems to me the most difficult writing of all, because it requires a convergence of rarely assembled qualities. You need talent, of course, the gift of invention. You need ingenuity, empathy, tenacity. You need a minimum of literary ability and sometimes even skill. You need a particular feeling for dialogue and a respectable technical baggage. As Tati said, you have to know *how* films are made. Otherwise you write in the void, in an ivory tower, and your writing, however elegant, will remain untranslatable. And you have to know what the things you write will cost.

In addition to facing these constraints, this obligatory passage through the hands of actors and technicians, you have to possess a particular quality which is difficult both to achieve and to maintain: a certain humility. Not only because the film will most often belong to the director, and his name alone will be glorified (or vilified), but also because the thumbed and dog-eared written work will finally be tossed aside like the caterpillar's skin. Somewhere along the way the screenwriter must be able to switch allegiances, transfer all his love to the film. So as he leaves the studio on the last day of shooting, he must be able to look at the wastebaskets without a hint of bitterness.

Tati and Suzanne kept me more than ten days in that dim room, ten days which I now think of as my coming of age. They showed me shots and reverse shots, establishing shots, different ways of centering, good and bad link shots. I learned the first echoes of a brand-new language. They talked about tempo and about style. A slender, lively young man with big glittering eyes often dropped in. He was Tati's assistant but also his gagwriter, musician, and magician. His name was Pierre

Etaix. It was with him that I would make my real start in film a few years later. We have never parted.

Pierre sat beside me and tried to answer my naive questions. Why was this particular shot not exactly as it was described in the screenplay? For all kinds of unforeseeable reasons, Pierre said: a jetty (this was in *Monsieur Hulot*) might be too short, an actor was having trouble coordinating his moves (which in comedy have to be super-precise), there was bad weather, a temperamental dog—all the hazards of shooting—or else the sudden realization that what made you laugh on paper turns heavy, or unbelievable, or seems telegraphed, when you try to give it shape and life for the camera.

These are accidents of passage. They are unavoidable. No matter what precautions you take, despite careful preparation, improvisations, amendments, rehearsals, there are certain *moments* (the only word I can find) which refuse to become parts of a film. You can of course try to force them, to manhandle them into the picture. They submit reluctantly, always leaving behind some sense of dissatisfaction in filmmakers and audiences.

Why is it that what seems right and proper when you read it, even when you read it aloud, becomes false and forced when you see it filmed? Is it the passage from our subjectivity as readers, in which the shapes we imagine necessarily remain vague, to the implacable objectivity of film, whose eye and whose heart are different from ours? Are we struggling with something irreducible here?

Every director has encountered this resistance, this recalcitrance. It is as if the scene, or a moment within a scene, digs in its heels like a rebellious mule. Despite all our tricks, this damned moment will not become part of the film.

Actors often feel it instinctively. They say, "I have a problem with this." They cannot define it too clearly, but at every attempt to dive into the scene they stumble. They are not at ease; they fake it.

For the alert director this is a danger signal. Careful: something is wrong. And he must resolve the perennial problem: should he compel the actor to conquer this resistance—and perhaps find a second truth beyond all his soul-searching—or should he at once modify the scene, even eliminate it?

Every metamorphosis of a screenplay, that is, every filming of situations dreamed up by the screenwriter, thus comes festooned with compromises that the writer hopes will be minor. A screenplay is always the dream of a film. You dream up the finest performers, the most beautiful settings, rivers of dollars, truly new images.

When it comes time to shoot, which is the first moment of truth (the other such moment will be the day of release), you almost always have to make do with what is at hand. The compromises begin. In fact, they have already begun in the preparatory stages: So-and-So is not available; there is not enough money to shoot the ocean-liner scene; no question of sending a crew to this or that country after the latest developments there; and, always, the pressure of time. They say that during the filming of *Les Enfants du Paradis* at the Victorine studios in Nice in 1944, Marcel Carné went into tantrums over American warplanes supporting the Allied landings in Provence. "Can't you go somewhere else?" the director yelled at the aircraft. "We're trying to make a film!"

Leaving aside such cases of the unexpected, compromises crowd in as soon as preparation begins. I often think that one of a director's prime gifts is the ability to choose among compromises: those he can live with, however reluctantly, in order to save the film; those that will have to be fought every inch of the way; and the ones he has to refuse no matter what.

The metamorphosis can sometimes reach absurd levels. I recall, in the 1960s, a director who decided to make a film based on the life of a desert monk, one of those saintly hermits whose miraculous deeds are a part of early Christian legend. He convinced a producer, who hired a screenwriter, and they went to work.

But after a few weeks they wondered: why should we keep this beautiful story locked away in ancient times? Couldn't we bring it closer to us, set it in the seventeenth century, for example? And why not in modern times, for that matter?

Of course, there are no longer miracle-working saints in modern times—not in the West, at any rate. Then could the story be set in India, in Africa, in South America perhaps? Here the producer had his own views. Not a chance of shooting in Africa or India. Audiences would not identify with an exotic character. No, the film must be made in Europe. Otherwise, there would be no film. (It is always this way; you are never given the choice between this film and another one which might be better; you have a choice of this film or no film at all.)

Fine. Where could a saint be found in Europe in the 1960s? Discussions dragged on for nearly a year before bearing fruit. It was decided that the nearest modern equivalent to a saint of Christianity's heroic period was a private eye. No doubt about that. Producer, screenwriter, and director were agreed. Thus did an original and perhaps harebrained idea (a saint! what kind of sense did that make?) collapse cozily and flaccidly into the weariest of all cinema clichés.

They made the film. A thriller set in Madrid, with Eddie Constantine in the lead role. I have to admit that the director who had proposed his farfetched idea a year earlier withdrew at the last moment. Someone else made the film. A mediocre film, a flop.

A few days after our first meeting, Jacques Tati took me to a recording studio. He was personally handling the sound effects for *My Uncle*. That afternoon he had to find the sound of a glass shattering on the floor of a modern kitchen. A thorough man, Tati had walled himself in behind a good thirty cases of glasses of varying quality, and for hours, one after the other, with the utmost gravity, he dropped these glasses on different types of floor—stone, wood, cement, tile, even metal. I watched him amazed, wondering if this long, boring, unsung work was what the cinema was supposed to be about. I followed Tati more or less everywhere, usually with Etaix, attending projections followed by long anxious discussions. ("Can we clearly see the dog's tail go past the electric eye that shuts the garage door? Yes? Clearly? You're sure people will see it?") He doubtless sensed that he should show me as much as possible before letting me write the book. From this comes the importance I have always accorded technical skill, the hardware of filming; sounds, lights, editing work. Starting out with only literary training, I have tried over the years to spend as much working time as possible on sets and in movie houses and laboratories. Throughout the shooting of Pierre Etaix's first film, *The Suitor,* I was prop man and boom operator. We were hardly overfinanced: indeed we were a skeleton crew.

But taking the sound as you follow a production, slipping the boom in among the lights without throwing shadows on the walls, giving an edge (even a slight one) to this or that sound, this or that voice, is all a part of the overall work. None of it is irrelevant to the writing. Even today, I spend as many hours as I can in research workshops. I ask to be initiated into the mysteries of synthetic imaging, holograms, all the latest extensions of the language of film.

In the approach to every technique, even the latest digital ones, there is an ancient secret. Every apprenticeship is a total process, changing not only our gestures and our ways of seeing but probably our whole being. A precise craftsman rarely harbors crazy ideas. He remains calm and sure of touch, even when away from his work. For us the real danger—and it often arises—would lie in believing that technique is enough, that virtuosity can supplant ideas.

Doubtless the opposite is true. The older I get the more I admire artists who conceal their technical prowess—like Renoir, Buñuel, Yasujiro Ozu—who carefully avoid effect, shun purple passages. That they are capable of every kind of virtuosity I do not doubt. But I like it when they aim for something else, a mystery, an essence, an enhancement of life, a less striking but rarer quality.

I am not attracted either by over-obvious painters (even though their work sometimes sets obscene records at public auctions) who flaunt their effects and often repeat themselves.

I like these words by Delacroix:

"If one lived a hundred years one would prefer Titian to all others. He is not the painter for young people. He is the least mannered and consequently the most varied of painters. . . . The least mannered artist has to be the most varied: he constantly defers to genuine emotion. He has to render that emotion. Embellishment and a vain show of facility or skill do not interest him. On the contrary, he disdains everything that does not lead him to a livelier expression of his thought."

In a screenplay, as elsewhere, you must be wary of technique, which can so quickly turn into mere fluency. You have to push forever further, toward "genuine emotion." Early on, with Tati and Etaix, I noticed that a large part of the function called writing consists precisely in not writing. The very act of writing is dangerous, for it carries with it a kind of time-honored prestige which is very often its only justification. It is written, therefore it is true; therefore I will do nothing more to it. When a screenplay is finished, many filmmakers call it "The Bible," as if it were Holy Writ.

And I have often noticed, during play rehearsals for instance, that if you give an actor a line orally, without writing it down, he treats it casually and often with fertile inventiveness. If you write the same line on a piece of paper, or better still type it, the actor at once respects it. It may even paralyze him.

When we left the studios, Tati would sit with me at a café terrace and we would watch passersby. Most didn't really catch our eye. But suddenly someone would appear, riveting us with some detail; a look, something special about clothes or body. This was our return to the source. You have to watch and *see,* and at once start imagining, move from passive to active, try to hang upon this chance encounter a story, a joke, a mishap, an accident that seems to fit that person. The whole street, the city, and—why not?—the wide world and all the planet's inhabitants seemed to exist just to give us the excuse for an immense comic film it was our business to discover.

I have long pursued this "work"—looking upon the world as a pretext for films—in all its different guises, with Pierre Etaix, Luis Buñuel, Milos Forman, and Peter Brook, among others. Of course, each of us sees only what suits his taste or interest. A man with a limp may seem funny or pitiful, depending on your eye. I recall Milos Forman on a café terrace, watching the coming and going of passersby and prostitutes at a Pigalle intersection and muttering disconsolately, "Only God could have directed this!" The essential thing is never to abandon contact with real life in favor of a cerebral construct. You must start out by exploring and taming what is around you before starting to impart all the necessary twists and turns to reality.

In 1968, Milos Forman decided to make a film in New York. As his leading character he chose a young runaway, a social dropout. There were many such runaways in those days, kids who suddenly left their dull families to join garish gypsy bands of hippies in the streets of the East Village, seeking another life, a better life. The Beatles had just written a wonderful song on the theme, "She's Leaving Home."

Milos asked me to work with him. I joined him in New York, which both of us were seeing for the first time. When you first arrive in the United States your reaction is always the same: "I know this country!" We have all seen and loved so many American films in our lives that everything is familiar—skyscrapers, Colorado, New York's yellow cabs, even the wail of police sirens. Our first visits to America all took place in movie houses.

When you actually visit, of course, some adjustments are necessary. New York in 1968 had surprises in store. Unprepared for the new ways, Milos and I were strangers in a land we found strange.

To acclimatize ourselves, we decided to live right in among our characters in Greenwich Village instead of shutting ourselves in some hotel room to "write" this film, which was called *Taking Off*. We walked around, ringing apartment doorbells at random, saying in our horrible accents, "We are two European filmmakers; we want to make a film about young Americans. Do you have children?"

No one slammed the door in our faces. Once a family even shared its meal with us. And the door of our little rental house on Leroy Street was always open to all comers. We listened for hours to their stories, which we initially had trouble understanding because of the kind of English they used, a tribal jargon designed for the exclusive use of group members (in fact, several scenes in the British version of the movie were subtitled so that English audiences would understand them).

The screenplay came only later, much later, after lengthy real-life immersion. In the end, most of the film's scenes were made up, like the one depicting an "Association of Parents of Runaway Children," which was so realistic that the producers received letters asking for the organization's address. But the invention was rooted in real life. It could never have existed without the exceptional cast of heart and mind that marked that period, and without our own intimate, persistent, anthropological approach.

It is best for the writing to come last, when the essential has already been found. As late as possible.

The second phenomenon to emerge (along with a certain hesitant surprise, which over the years takes on many forms but never ceases to be a surprise) is the growth of the imagination. The imagination is a real muscle, which like memory is strengthened by exercise. But unlike memory, which we believe—or did believe until recently—to be located in a particular area of the brain, no one is sure precisely where the imagination holds court. It is in the head, of course, but also in the body, the senses, the nerves, the reflexes. There it is, more or less lively, depending on age and character, wanting only to unfold, to spread, to bloom. It lives in us under the most mysterious guises; it makes our dreams and our daydreams its own; it is the wind swelling our sails, it is our life transformed.

We all know that we imagine. If we didn't, our lives would be too real. As soon as life's hubbub dies down, even if only for a few minutes, we rediscover this secret companion. Our imagination takes the helm, moving in subtly and gently, taking advantage of this momentary inaction, this return to self, to raise the invisible curtains within us. It sets us down before a stage on which an actor stands. That actor is ourselves. Stage and auditorium are one. Building on bits and pieces of reality, of what we encounter every day, of our friends, of men or women we desire, we enter another world.

Trying to look casual, some of us press on a little farther and try to make others share the pictures, sounds, and stories that flow through us. Calling ourselves professional storytellers, we organize the errant, daydreaming part of ourselves, put it to work, manhandle and harry it: treatment it both loathes and loves.

As experience succeeds experience, we become aware of this tenant. Fairly soon—a first reason for surprise—we see that its possibilities for exploration seem limitless. Its territory is unimaginably vast and grows daily. The number of situations which the imagination— an untrammeled imagination—can conceive of may well approach a notional infinite. Details, looks, movements, words: no limits. In the nineteenth century some people believed there was a finite number of dramatic situations. At most a few dozen. Nothing could be less accurate than this narrowly arithmetical view of our imaginary world. Everything can be drama, action, story, romance, as long as interest is maintained and our listeners sit wide-eyed instead of fleeing.

Many are the seeds planted over the years in our furrows. The storytellers of Africa, India, and Persia are truly inexhaustible. But from time to time, particularly in France, home-grown tyrants of reductionism have arisen, axe in hand, to declare: this is how you must write. This way, and no other. They have burned poets at the stake. In seventeenth-century France, for example, classical order advanced step by step with absolute monarchy to fall pitilessly upon the delectable, baroque, priceless, mystical, and obscene poetic blossoming of the first third of the century. Upon poets named Chausson, or Le Petit.

Enough of this calamitous disorder, say the tyrants. We must now respect the rules, express ourselves clearly. Only propriety counts. Let us yet again reduce, with the connivance of good taste. The result was that for the whole of the next century, the eighteenth, no one wrote a single poem in France. Mountains of verse, but not one poem.

This danger, always the same although in different forms, permanently threatens us. We are all of us, whatever our occupation, drawn to filing cabinets, pigeonholes, labels, drawers. What could be safer than to duck down the first little side street, so sheltered, so cozy, so easy to get to know? What could be safer than established forms (which we are pleased to call classicism)? We have said nothing yet and already we are beginning to repeat ourselves.

We make lots of films; maybe we no longer create cinema at all. We have lost the spirit of invention, the spirit of adventure. When a vague reproach from our shadow regions annoys us, we justify ourselves with one word: fidelity. We say and believe that we are faithful to ourselves. Yet fidelity is a word like so many others; it means precisely nothing, at least when you use it on its own. Fidelity to what? By remaining faithful to form, we often betray essence. And even form will die later, long since drained of all substance.

We have only imagination to rescue us from oblivion,

to haul us out of our rut. Without our knowing it, it is always there, returning again and again to the attack, and with unfailing grace. How could we stop imagining? Imagination carries us effortlessly through every looking-glass; it sings with a siren voice. At every step it is there to help us flee the monotonous loop of things already seen and heard, of expertise, of dangerous experience. It opens up unsuspected paths through the undergrowth.

Naturally it is sometimes frightened, for it is under constant threat. Since it can dream up anything, turn the world upside down, put the beggar on the throne and boot the king into a ditch, since it can even dream up apocalypse, the end of all things, supreme nothingness, imagination is hedged about with mistrust. So it is ill-treated, locked up. Regularly thwarted, it often shrinks back into the darkest depths of its lair. In some people—we have only to look around us—it seems to have disappeared, to have been murdered by routine and by fear. So many people are forever locked into rigid living, into closed thinking.

No doubt the great danger, in the screenwriter's field as in others, is believing that expertise is enough. But the truth is that he has to provoke it constantly, upset it, work on each film as if it were his first.

Buñuel read the paper every day. He read it for news of the world, which interested him; and he read it to hear about our work. Reading and commenting on the press was part and parcel of our research for a screenplay. This habit could induce irritation, sometimes even panic. One day we read that a bomb had exploded in Paris's Sacré-Coeur basilica. The report electrified us, for we had just dreamed up (for *That Obscure Object of Desire*) a terrorist group claiming to act in the name of Baby Jesus.

Next morning, full of anxiety, we opened the paper to find out what the inquiry had yielded. Not another word. Other news had swallowed the basilica. It is always deflating when reality is served to you by the press. The great bulk of that day's news held no interest for us; the item that fascinated us had vanished suddenly and forever.

That is why reality is not enough. The imaginary must graft itself onto reality, must distort it, strengthen it.

I remember another morning. Buñuel came in looking pale and worried. I asked him what was wrong. "Everything's finished," he said. "There's really no point in going on working. The end of the world is just about here." I asked him why he was so alarmed.

"Haven't you read the paper?" he replied. "Two Swiss bankers committed suicide on the same day!"

Yet the world went on, the next day and the days that followed. A disappointment, perhaps.

Another part of our work was telling one another our dreams every morning. If we had forgotten them we—or at least I—would make them up. I kept in mind André Breton's words about a man he didn't like: "He's a swine. He never dreams."

Newspapers, then dreams: our sum of the everyday. And this of course was supplemented through the long hours of the day by reflection, improvisation, and invention, to which we were bound by contract. A rambling and loosely organized kind of intellectual inquiry which

165

could sometimes get utterly lost in childhood memories or stories about a mutual friend, in pictures seen and things read, and which could be broken by long silences in which each of us could, or almost could, like Edgar Allan Poe, gropingly follow the other's thoughts. It could all disintegrate into laughter, even quarrels; and then suddenly, out of nowhere, a scene would materialize and was hurried indoors and tidied up. We moved tables, chairs, and lights around to make a rudimentary set, and we began to act, making things up as we went, over and over, three times, six times, ten times. At each run-through, words and movements grew sharper. And out of this disordered activity something was born. Very soon I would start to take notes so as not to forget this phrase or that movement, born of improvisation—of the kind it is often impossible to recall later on.

Sometimes such a road leads nowhere. Scenes lapse into silence, discouragement. You return to your waiting. You tell yourself that you will never come up with anything worthwhile, anything that will be wholly satisfactory to both of you. You call the waiter and order a coffee. You go back to the papers, to this or that story that has already been covered several times. You look out at the landscape, which hasn't changed. You're a couple of insects seeking a way out of a jar. There is a secret exit somewhere, a way out to vast open spaces.

Agitation, shot through with real spells of boredom. The strangest of activities, impossible to describe.

As for training the imagination, the muscle which makes the essential breakthroughs, we did a daily exercise that required real discipline. For a half-hour, at the end of every afternoon's work, I would stay alone in my room while Buñuel made his solitary way to the bar—his holy of holies, preferably peopled by shadows—and ordered his evening cocktail.

Thus separated, each of us committed himself to inventing, in half an hour, a story. It could be short or long, present or past, sad or slapstick, or even just a detail, a joke. Once this was done, I joined him in the bar and we traded discoveries. They could be related to the screenplay of the moment, or not—it didn't matter. The point was to keep the imagination on its toes, to force it to arouse itself at the very hour—the end of the day—when it tends to doze off.

As I entered the bar I could tell from Luis's face whether he was pleased or let down by his day's discovery. And this ability was probably mutual, for every face lights up at the onset of a good idea.

Sometimes, earlier in the day, as we struggled with a tricky scene which nothing seemed to resolve, he would say, "Perhaps it'll come to me tonight, with the help of gin."

You cannot advise everyone in search of an idea to seek out a snug and peaceful bar, slowly drink a dry martini, and let things take their course. For some it wouldn't work. But there isn't the slightest doubt that for Buñuel it was fertile ground. With the slow warmth of the alcohol rising in him, he said, he felt movements in the air, saw fleeting images, he even saw characters slide silently from one bar stool to the next.

From Jacques Tati's café terrace to the dim bar where Buñuel waited for me, there were countless such propitious places. I have written scenes of the *Mahabharata* stuck in Madras traffic jams, or else waiting with

167

Peter Brook in a regional airport in India for a plane that might or might not land. On the other hand, there are imaginations that are capricious and even compulsive, insisting, for example, on the presence of the color red, or flute music, or excessive heat, or the sound of surf. Reading the requirements of writers, including screenwriters, you are tempted to believe you are thumbing through a catalog of serious deviants. I knew one screenwriter capable of being driven over the edge by the sound of just one bird. Fetishism? A mask for laziness? An unpleasant distant memory, some trauma?

Who knows. Fortunately, such things are not much studied.

What seems more or less certain is that the field is truly limitless. You can set up obstacles in it, of course. You can also wander in it aimlessly and get lost. You can plow the field any way you choose. But plow it you must. Anyone can dream of a film needing no care. But he must not be surprised if prudent visitors avoid it.

So plowing is essential. But so is benign neglect, so is leaving the land fallow. You can abandon a story for weeks, months, years perhaps. No matter: its life does not necessarily come to a halt. A long and invisible process goes on without your knowledge. You must allow it to exist, grant yourself moments of rest, of lotus-eating, of woolgathering. A part of you stays awake. And one of these days, if all goes well, you will harvest the fruits.

Those of us who toil in this obscure area learn that human imagination is perfectly innocent, and that we should constantly struggle against our own prohibitions. Contrary to what religion has dinned into us over the centuries, there is no "sinful thought," no "crime of intent." On the contrary, we must welcome everything, imagine everything. The screenwriter (when he is inventing) is entitled and probably required to be vulgar, odious, bigoted, and exploitative, a loathsome potential criminal. Several times a day he must kill his father, rape his mother, sell his sister, and betray his country. Letting all barriers melt away, forcing himself to wear an absurd or unpleasant mask, he has to seek out the criminal within, or the man of bad taste, or the man he hates, the man he wouldn't for anything in the world try to be.

Rest assured, he will find them all.

Just as a theoretical or didactic approach at the outset of a project can mask fatal dangers (nothing is so easy or so incapacitating as theory), so self-censorship, recoiling in fear, or refusing to see oneself whole are acts of castration, transgressions, assaults on the imagination that will sooner or later exact their toll.

Not only must the screenwriter learn to look into his own dark depths during the very act of writing, but he must have the courage to show himself to his partner. He must have the courage to suggest this or that particular idea, stubbornly arguing its soundness even though he also realizes it is dangerous, even vile, even disgusting. He must submit to an unending exercise in shamelessness in order to lose his fear of the judgment of others, to drop the cloak of respectable aloofness behind which he hides like a timid fish.

For he never works alone, even when there is no one else there. He is himself multiple. If there is a more or less well-disguised swine inside him, there is also an ascetic and a dove. All of them will act and react. It is inevitable. The swine will not be allowed to write the screenplay all on his own.

A film is complete when the screenplay has vanished. Its structure has faded from view. All the audience's intelligence focuses on the film itself, not on the way the film was made. Of course, you can announce (as Jean-Luc Godard sometimes did) that the film itself is "a film in the making," a process we are supposed to witness and share (but since cinema is not immediate, like theatre, what Godard proposes is just another form of illusion). Otherwise, all the preparatory work disappears. All the joints, all the necessary information injected as the work progressed, are now assimilated into the action itself. The scaffolding has melted away.

Now every image and every word surprises us. Suddenly everything is unexpected. Yet at the same time it all seems inevitable. Everything has led up to it. It is what we had secretly striven to achieve. In these privileged, astonishing, and essential first moments, the film embodies and gives clear shape to our original desire, affording it a satisfaction which is the livelier for being unexpected, undreamed-of.

And in the hope (often dashed but springing eternal) of attaining such moments, we must learn to rid ourselves gently (remember Titian and Delacroix) of the technical skill we have so laboriously acquired. Buñuel used to call it "the fix-all." A too-glittering discovery, too glitteringly displayed, can shatter the audience's intimate bond with a film. It can disconnect us, just like the actor who comes onstage dazzlingly costumed, or the excessively resplendent set which elicits our admiring gasp.

For then our admiration is directed at the beauty of that one image, a beauty detached and isolated from the film itself. It is a beauty that has without our knowledge disconnected us, the beauty of an image or the flash and glitter of words.

Peter Brook tells about a popular British stage actor who used to raise a hand to let audiences know that a witty line was on its way. Watch out, here it comes, this is a good one! In their own way, many filmmakers do the same thing, half the time without even realizing it. But what I call the "meat of the film" is located beyond words and images, in the indefinable realm of feeling, of the vital bond linking human beings, in that secret sumptuous nourishment whose absence invariably leaves bus hungry.

In a screenplay the requisite disappearance of the skeleton of the story, the erasure of visible effects, has only one goal: to transform invention into apparent reality. To give life and truth to what is born of whim and a slow breaking-in process. The imagination must do its work and then metamorphose, give up its glitter and sometimes its personal arrogance; it must act as if it were no longer there, having yielded its place to reality. It must return to its dark lair to await the next offensive.

So it conquers by disappearing. It is like raw material that has vanished into thin air, still present but impalpable. Here we are probably at the secret heart of the machinery. There is not much we can say about it.

171

We are in the presence of the triumph of what is no longer seen. It is like those years of stubborn practice that pave the way for the athlete's few simple moves when the day of competition arrives.

The screenplay is not only the dream of a film but its infancy. It goes through a toddling, stammering phase, gradually discovering its strengths and its weaknesses. As it gains confidence it begins to move under its own power, once again recalling Peter Brook's formless hunch which sharpens and grows stronger day by day.

But a film can also age and be snapped up by death. This will be a natural death if the film has simply ceased to interest us, if our memory rejects it, turns away from it. We rightly say that it has become unwatchable. Some films may even be stillborn, unseen from the moment of their birth and forever after.

But it can also be accidental death—when earthquake or fire (like the one in Mexico City's Cinemateca in 1982) destroys rare copies, or when one of those mysterious corrosion phenomena occurs, attacking film in the heart of the bunkers protecting it.

In this progression from the potential to the actual, from the dream film or infant film to the aware, adult film, the screenwriter learns to withdraw gradually from the adventure. In the first months he is the master. The film belongs to him. He knows all its twists and turns; sometimes he is the only one to see it.

Then they decide to start shooting, and he has to relinquish power. The project gets away from him. It has to move into other hands in order to live.

It is a risky transition. To avoid any break, any radical or heretical change of tone, the director should be close to the screenwriter from the beginning, working with him from the very start. Thus, even at this early stage, the film will also be the director's, which it will be in the credits and history books anyway. The transition will have been more natural, with fewer jolts and scars. Director and screenwriter will have grown accustomed together to the child they are expecting.

Together, without even realizing it, they will have invented images, heard phrases and sounds. This first aspect of the film belongs to them both.

When we worked together, Buñuel often asked me to draw scenes from the film, which I did alone in my room at night. The next day, before I showed him my drawings, we did a rapid check of how we saw things. I would ask, for instance, "Where's the door in the parachute scene?"

He at once answered, "On the left."

"The mistress of the house?"

"On the right, by the couch."

And so on, almost always in agreement. It happened hundreds of times. Even though we sat opposite one another—his right being my left and vice versa—we had the same vision of the general arrangement of the set, of the characters' positions. As our discussions and improvisations developed, an inner form took residence in us, like a secret lodger, a form ultimately stronger than the geographic arrangement of the hotel room we worked in. We were indeed already in the same film together.

* * *

In the 1950s, with a few notable exceptions (Robert Bresson, Tati, Jean Renoir, Jacques Becker), screenwriters dominated the French cinema. The director's function was generally limited to putting the story into pictures, a technical but demanding formality. All films looked alike. The only difference was in the stories they told.

The form seemed forever fixed—in France and elsewhere.

This seductive adversary (which tells us "respect the rules of art and you will all be artists") is called formalism. It puts form first; it insists on seeing all things through this imposed screen. Eisenstein denounced it most energetically—and sometimes fell prey to it.

Starting in the late 1950s, the New Wave violently overthrew formalism and monotony. Above all else, the new filmmakers insisted that every film bear the stamp of its author, that this author necessarily be the director, and that in consequence something definite must happen when shooting starts. This call to arms rang through the world. An explosion of styles, of genres, and even of shooting techniques followed—and all this at a time when television, the new monster, was insidiously challenging the supremacy of cinemas, those palaces of the people that we had believed would stand forever.

The new conception naturally tossed the screenwriter into oblivion. He was no longer needed. The director, promoted to sole "author," staked exclusive claim to the terrain. The screenwriter became a suspect and probably dangerous character, a subspecies among writers, a failed novelist capable only of a tireless rehashing of his necessarily mediocre recipes.

So we the audience were subjected to a fearsome

avalanche of intimate narcissistic works, recollections, little fantasies, poetic effusions, greeting-card messages; we were even shown the director himself in the modish throes of creation.

But these too were unwatchable films, since they addressed themselves only to the director himself and a few of his acolytes. The essential ingredient, contact with others, was lost.

Already exposed to television's increasingly seductive wiles, audiences naturally fled these vaporous films, which rotted on the shelves. By the end of the 1960s the screenplay was back. Quick, quick, tell us a story! The need was desperate.

All balancing acts are difficult, for they work only once. Everything has to be reinvented daily. The shared journey of a screenwriter and a director is like a love story. You have to feel your way blindly, seeking common ground, common likes and dislikes. When Buñuel saw me for the first time at a lunch in Cannes, the first question he asked me, looking straight into my eyes— and I sensed that the question was a deep, serious one that might decide our life together—was:

"Do you drink wine?"

When I said yes, adding that I came from a family of winegrowers, his features relaxed, he smiled at me, he called the wine waiter. At least we shared that taste. Later, of course, we discovered others.

When I meet a director with whom I am committed to spending several months of my life, I always ask myself: what film does he hope to make? I might as well get an idea now, since in any case he is the one who will be making it. Sometimes he does not yet know. He too sees nothing but a vague shape, which together we will try to bring into the open.

And so, out of those first hesitant moves, discoveries, false starts, out of those early moments of pleasure and of strife, out of jealousies, misunderstandings, a little boredom, much pessimism, a betrothal results. The question to be avoided at all costs, I believe—as with any promising couple—is who will be the dominant partner. It is of no importance. This is not a contest, and the audience doesn't care.

A minor personal victory ("I won, I got him to agree to my idea!") is senseless. It can even be a defeat for the film, and the film alone counts.

There are moments when the screenwriter is deeply, honestly convinced that his idea is right, that he is justified in fighting for it, but how can one be sure one is being honest with oneself, that self-esteem is totally out of the picture? We are, all of us, utterly convinced that our taste and judgment are the best in the world. How do we quell that inner presumption of superiority which makes our ideas look better than those of others?

How are we to focus only on the work in hand? How are we to rein in our appetite for glory, money, and power?

Buñuel often said that films should be like cathedrals. The authors' names should be removed from the credits, leaving just a few anonymous reels, pure, free of any trace of their creator. Then we would watch them the way we enter a cathedral, not knowing the names of those who built it, or even the master builder.

But the path taken by films—and by every other medium—leads in the opposite direction. Dogged by critics, hounded by packs of hairsplitting historians, the creator has been increasingly thrust to the fore. He can even count for more than his work (in Van Gogh's case there is no room for doubt), so more and more a work's creator is in the limelight. The first thing you look for in a painting today is the signature. It is the spirit of the times: we turn artists into media stars.

A screenwriter has to make do. He must accept the fact that the public gives the director credit for ideas and intentions that are often his own. Basically, as we know full well, it is all just a matter of vanity. Even true fame, that superannuated romantic notion, is a little suspect in the climate of our times.

The wound is not fatal, and we take comfort where we can.

What happens between two or more people who work together? Nobody is quite sure. We don't even know what goes on within ourselves at the moment of creation. We feel inside us, perhaps, a miniature theatre at work, in which we are both actors and audience (although it's an audience naturally disposed to be indulgent). We want to like what "it" offers us. Most often it wins us over even before it starts—unless, on the contrary, our critical spirit is so ferocious that it makes us hiss at everything our imagination begets. Some authors are instantly delighted by everything they invent, while others remain forever dissatisfied. Both attitudes are harmful and incapacitating.

This step-by-step discovery of a theme, a story, a style—a highly erratic process, marked by long dry spells and sudden flashes—closely resembles the work of an actor venturing into a part. What will he find? At first he has no idea. A play—by Shakespeare, say, or Chekhov—always presents a vibrant and indefinable whole, impervious to the most piercing analysis. It is out of the question to tackle those plays as if they were the expression of a particular point of view. To do so would mean stifling them, strangling them, the eternal pitfall of limited directors, who invariably force their own terms on anything which is beyond their comprehension.

During rehearsals for one of Pirandello's plays, a high-strung actress said to the playwright, "Maestro, I fail to understand. On page twenty-seven my character says this. On page fifty-four she says that. Can it be possible, given everything that has happened to her, her motives, her character, that she has changed so much, that she can say such a thing after having clearly said . . ."

Pirandello patiently heard her out (he was a polite man). She spoke at length, asking the usual questions. When she finally stopped he said, as if it were obvious, "But why are you asking me all this? I am the author."

It seems right, despite the apparent paradox, because a true author never knows exactly what he meant. He scarcely knows what he said. He is what Victor Hugo called "the mouth of darkness." Words are transmitted through him, often quite beyond his control. They come from obscure regions; the richer and deeper his genius, the vaster those regions will be. They are regions he shares with others, and even, in the case of the greatest authors, with all humankind, for he becomes one of humanity's voices.

Here I would like to interject a few words from Martin Buber: "We must lose the sense of self. We must listen only for the Word speaking into a person's ear.

As soon as we start to hear our own voice we must be silent."

Here we have moved far beyond the concept of the *author's film.*

Pirandello's answer was right for another reason: it was an elegant way of telling the actress, "But that is your job, my dear. You are paid to find the road from page twenty-seven to page fifty-four. You are committed to finding it. And you have a director to guide you."

But there must always be a clear stretch at the start of rehearsals. There must be minimal understanding if the actor is not to launch wildly into the blue. "No point in getting excited before we know why," Peter Brook tells actors who seek the easy way out in excessive emotional display. A calm approach and a lucid and thoughtful reading are helpful, if only in laying bare what is vague or contradictory in the writing, what is likely to cause difficulty.

But the most serious, the most pernicious illusion—and here the actor's and the author's paths converge, in film as on the stage—is when we convince ourselves that the intellectual approach is enough, that intelligent analysis will cover every contingency. All that is needed, we tell ourselves, is for the author to know what he means, draw up a precise plan, define his structures—and the rest will follow. In which case the actor's performance, too, would simply be a translation into words and gestures of an idea the mind has already chewed over.

The mind fosters its own illusion that it can know, understand, analyze, and invent anything. The effects of this illusion are dangerous and subtle, the more so because the ordinary instruments of this intellectual quest (thought, reflection, introspection) in a sense work upon themselves. Thus thought permanently secretes its own illusion, which is the belief that it thinks, and in consequence that it knows ("I know Mexico, I know Shakespeare": very usual illusions). Just as consciousness (to adopt other terminology) easily persuades itself that it is wakeful, attentive, free.

Or more accurately, thought—the actor's, the author's, anyone's—imagines it can distinguish itself from itself. It thinks it can examine itself from the outside as a discrete, static object, whereas it is exactly the opposite: indistinct, shifting, vague.

Since we believe (or neurologists assert) that the human brain, that prodigious organ, is also a great idle blob which delights in simplifications and reductions, a dullwitted prodigy quite ready to applaud the first witty (or noisy) phrase it encounters, the pitfalls lying in wait for both author and actor are legion. Our brain likes to seduce itself, to outwit itself, like a conjurer astonished by his own skill and honestly assuming that he is a real miracle-worker, even applauding himself at the end of his act.

Our brain—our mind, if you prefer—is ever ready for self-worship, ever ready to adore whatever springs from its own depths. It no longer realizes that it is at once adorer and adored, that it is both instrument and obstacle.

Sooner or later we will have to escape it, abandon intelligence and its tricks. Both author and actor must pierce through to the next zone, or next zones, those which analysis can neither penetrate nor define, the dark zones where true mystery dwells.

180

At a certain stage understanding ceases. It has to. Beneath it (or above, or all around: clearly such spatial concepts have no meaning) we must let things go, we must not try to probe those life-generating mists. For real life, whole life, is there, in that constant back-and-forth movement from light to darkness, from light to the little-known and boundless jungle we can explore only through action and play.

Back and forth between exploration and reflection, between the light and darkness, between fallow and plowed.

In the same way, work on a screenplay often operates in a series of waves. The first waves are exploratory. We open all the doors and we begin to seek, neglecting no path, no blind alley. The imagination launches unbridled into a hunt which can lead it into the vulgar, the absurd, the grotesque, which can even make the imagination forget the theme that is the object of the hunt.

Whereupon another wave rears, surging in the opposite direction. This is the backwash, the withdrawal to what is reasonable, essential, to the old question: exactly why are we making this and not some other film? Quite simply, what basically interests us here?

This is the moment when, like Pirandello's agitated actress, we survey the road the characters have traveled; but we also look at verisimilitude, structure, interest, levels of audience understanding. By backtracking, by returning to our original garden, we obviously abandon along the way the majority of our illusory conquests— but not necessarily all of them. We return to scholarly, sometimes commonplace and even pettifogging concerns. They help us take stock: in the heat of the chase we might easily have forgotten to bring along our supplies, our drinking water, our maps.

Rare are the authors who can afford, on their own, this balanced and impartial movement between the two zones. But a working partnership, with the director for example, can make it possible.

The two seemingly opposing waves are complementary. There is no such thing as a screenplay launched in a total vacuum. At the very least you have to allow for the film's duration and the available budget. You must also take stock at every step: are the characters ahead of the audience or lagging behind? There is no point in laying the groundwork for a surprise if the audience has already guessed everything. And audiences guess a great deal. Where, we must ask, is our elusive and hypothetical audience at this stage of our story? Is it still interested in what we are telling it? Or has it already left the theatre, or switched channels? Is this scene clear enough or do we have to weigh it down a little? Does everyone know this word? Will we recognize this setting again after seeing it only once before, by night? Will we get permission to shoot on the Eiffel Tower? Is this line too long, or too enigmatic? Chekhov made an unforgettable observation: "It is best to avoid describing a mood. We must try to make it understandable through the hero's actions." Are we remaining strictly faithful to this ideal?

On the other hand, a screenplay that simply answered these questions would be no more than a meticulous bureaucratic exercise. It is timely breakthroughs, engineered by the imagination (or in the actor's case by improvisation), that shake things up, ignite, exalt.

The quest is never-ending. But every now and then,

actor and author have the feeling that the two waves have met. Something has surged forth. A union has been achieved.

This union, dazzling and ephemeral, can leave the actor in a kind of stupor as he walks off-stage.

It leaves the author equally stupefied. He too is double, triple, at times multiple. Instead of separating and compartmentalizing, he is welding different levels together. He is at once consciousness and unconsciousness, order and randomness. He is unceasing motion that can even seem aberrant and gratuitous, he is a quest.

Life as we ordinarily perceive it is confused and even incoherent. We walk down a street, we hear snatches of sentences, we see people of whom we know nothing performing actions whose significance eludes us. We perceive sounds without even hearing them, smells, colors flashing by; we feel heat, or cold, or the fatigue that comes from carrying a heavy burden uphill. Every one of these feelings can predominate turn by turn, depending on the individual, the mood, the moment.

Writing a story or a screenplay means injecting order into this disorder: making a preliminary selection of sounds, actions, and words; discarding most of them, then stressing and reinforcing the material selected. It means violating reality (or at least what we perceive of reality) to rebuild it in another way, confining the images within a given frame, selecting the real—voices, emotions, and sometimes ideas.

Even if this inescapable selection is not made until the editing stage, this is the precise moment when artifice enters the picture, whatever we do to resist or deny it. Better to acknowledge it, accept it, and yield to that second reality which is often more real, more compact, and sharper than the one we first saw in the disorder of the streets.

Conversely, a last barrier of mistrust is essential—for both actor and author are widely considered to possess *inspiration, passion, enthusiasm,* even *madness.* In fact, these so-called poetic states usually proceed not from an expansion but from a shrinking of the self. They are the product of willing blindness. In everyday working reality, nothing justifies them. Instead of succumbing, of yielding to the flow, we should avoid them as we would a mood-enhancing drug, the kind that would have us adoring whatever we produced.

I remember those thousands of poets in the late 1960s who smoked fat joints or took hashish and then wrote exultantly through the night, deeply convinced of their genius. When they read their work by the cold light of day, it all seemed woefully lifeless. Their heads throbbing, they were the first to agree. The same with cocaine. The difficulty is to find the real excitement within you while only sporadically losing your judgment.

Spontaneity, sincerity, self-searching: three more meaningless words. They are always used in connection with supposed virtues; they even carry a moral connotation (it is *good* to be spontaneous and sincere, it is *bad* to be a shrewd tactician). Only fairly long experience and a particular mindset—neither prudish nor aloof, but devoid of exhibitionism—allow you to let a scene come to you, to live it, improvise it, to let yourself be briefly taken over by a factor outside your ken, to give free rein to voice and body without losing vital control. In the best moments (rare, always unexpected), it all comes together. Nothing stands apart. Contradictions are swallowed up. You are no longer switching back and forth but advancing on a united front.

Swift miracles.

The screenwriter works hemmed in by a throng of technical constraints and commercial demands. He commits himself to a project that must necessarily be transformed beyond all recognition. Denied the novelist's comfortable introspection, he is usually required to describe his characters from the outside in. He knows his work is doomed to disappear; he himself is usually unknown to audiences, even by name. He therefore spends much of his life asking, "How can I ever give expression to who I am? How can I—like other, better-known artists—make my voice heard as well?"

Yet Flaubert fought with might and main for the opposite, for the total eclipse of the author. He unreservedly admired the independent, objective existence of Shakespeare's work, which is unmarked by its maker's heart and hand.

You can study Shakespeare your whole life long, yet the man he was will always slip through your fingers. His work tells us everything, and of him we know nothing. Was he a right- or left-winger? Garrulous or closemouthed? Did he prefer town to country? Women to men? No answer.

The peerless author is hidden in his characters, to
whom he has given the best of himself and who in their
turn express every feeling under the sun. He is the great
and authentic voice of the shadows. With him, the unseen triumphs. Supreme irony: the summit of glory
is namelessness. And the most personal voice of all is
everyman's.

The screenwriter, a cog in the film machine, believes
himself gagged, shunted aside, very often betrayed. People constantly, irritatingly, ask him, "Why don't you
write something personal?"

As if the words *something personal* possessed superior virtue, inhabited loftier levels of existence, as if it
were more important to be personal than useful, as if
once again, by some strange twist, only the author
counted, not his work.

Yet the screenwriter is the first to know, or at least to
guess (on certain days), that the notion of personal-at-all-
costs work sputtered out long ago, that no book and no
film exists unless it speaks to others, that an author de-
voting himself exclusively to gilding his image or bloat-
ing his bank account would swiftly dry up and disappear.

The screenwriter exists only to transmit certain feelings from one person to another. He is today's storyteller,
pursuing an ancient tradition with modern means. The
Berber speaking and singing on the public square in
Marrakesh plies the same trade I do. To those who listen
to him, the stories he strings together are necessary. "We
must listen to stories," someone says in the *Mahabharata*. "It is pleasant, and sometimes it makes us better."

Like earthworms burrowing through garden soil to
fertilize it, stories burrow from one person to the next

and sometimes from one people to the next. The route these stories take is unpredictable, but they carry a priceless cargo. What they say is told only by them.

An old Arab allegory depicts the storyteller as a man standing on a rock and addressing the ocean. He scarcely has time to drink a glass of water between stories. The sea listens, spellbound. One story follows another.

And the allegory adds: "If one day the storyteller falls silent, or someone silences him, no one can say what the ocean will do."

TRIMS

O nce a film has taken its final shape, discarded strips of film of varying length remain in the cutting room. They have found no place in the finished work and will probably disappear. We call them "trims." Here, before they can vanish beyond hope of recall, are some of mine.

Not shown: in *Casablanca,* in *Morocco,* not a single real Moroccan. The white presence rules. We are at home; we have brought our Western problems along in our Western luggage. The natives are insignificant bystanders, reduced to background, almost superfluous. And a closer look reveals that they are whites in makeup. Conclusion: Africa is us.

Compare this with certain vast seventeenth-century

canvases, for instance Lebrun's *The Battles of Alexander*. Savage fighting, on the widest of screens, but never a drop of blood.

The power of the not-seen. Laurel slips a raw egg into Hardy's pocket and then gives the pocket a slap. Hardy, who has put up no resistance, pokes his pocket open with a finger and peers inside.

We do not see what he sees. We do not need to. Why film a crushed egg in a jacket pocket? What we imagine is stronger, and above all funnier.

Frequently used effects: a car we hear crashing, a cake falling from a table into a diner's lap, a monster in the eyes of a screaming woman.

Resisting the temptation to show. Up to what point, though?

The influence—inadequately explored (how could we explore it?)—of film on reading. Does it help us see? We cannot tell for sure. Inevitably, people fit the faces of well-known actors to Balzac's characters. For years, Gérard Philipe represented a sort of ideal, omnipresent, all-purpose film incarnation of characters from Corneille to Stendhal for French audiences.

The star homogenizes. He prevents us from seeing the individual, the character. He is a mask; we see only him. Often he doesn't reveal but conceals.

* * *

In the 1970s in Prague I encountered a "human movie." He knew several banned films by heart (he had seen them abroad). People invited him to dinner; after the meal the guests made a circle and he "told" them the movie—that evening it was *The Discreet Charm of the Bourgeoisie*—forgetting not a single scene, not a single line. Shades of *Fahrenheit 451*.

A dialogue-writing exercise: give voices to characters. It can verge on madness. Who is speaking? Through whose mouth? Each character has to have his own voice, yet each of these voices is also the author's. The unending minuet! In *Les Enfants du Paradis*, Arletty, Pierre Renoir, and Louis Salou, all from different social backgrounds, use neither the same syntax nor the same vocabulary. Yet all of them speak Prévert.

What initially struck people about film was its ability to depict reality. In 1914 an American essayist whose name I forget said that compared to film, painting was "ridiculous caricature." Primo Levi has noted how difficult description is in novels, whereas in film everything seems simple. To show, you just turn the camera on.

But to show what? Reality? A flat image of reality? Are we really sure that a description by Balzac, in which reality is sifted through a screen of words, is not denser and deeper and finally more palpable than a slow panoramic shot across the same objects?

Is the eye truly supreme?

Jean-Claude Carrière

* * *

Film (they say) is a popular art form that now seems restricted to a dwindling audience of filmmakers and filmgoers. No one can really say why. Perhaps because, in television, the cinema has met an even more popular challenger. But this is not certain. Nor, I believe, is the game over.

In most countries, particularly in the Third World (with the exception of India, China, and Iran), it is getting harder, chiefly for economic reasons, to make films. The North American audiovisual industry has launched an all-out war. It seeks worldwide monopoly. Many countries didn't wake up to this in time and failed to protect themselves. Today, despite its vast potential market, starting a film company in a country like Brazil is an almost inevitable prelude to heroic failure.

American films, or rather American audiovisual products, movies and TV combined, are spreading across the globe and slowly annihilating local production.

This conquest is in fact a reconquest. In the early 1920s Hollywood enjoyed a near-monopoly on the manufacture of motion pictures, accounting for some eighty percent of world production. This percentage dropped in the following decades with the rise of foreign motion-picture industries and the outbreak of the Second World War, which cut a large swath of territories off from American distribution.

In 1945 the reconquest began. Its aims were clear

and openly acknowledged. Its promoters consider film a consumer product like any other, of no particular cultural importance. They pursue their massive program of re-conquest with every weapon that comes to hand. They have even been known to give certain television series to Brazilian and Russian networks, virtually free of charge.

It is a rational enterprise aimed at depriving all other countries, across the board, of their cinematic voice. "Movies are us," runs the American message, clear-eyed and uncompromising. "Why don't you make something else?"

Perhaps to skirt the kind of name-calling trap that sees Americans routinely stigmatized as "imperialists" and the French as "chauvinists," we should recall that our opposing viewpoints, which clashed along a broad front during the recent GATT talks, are rooted in separate but parallel traditions.

The Anglo-Saxon tradition is the older of the two. It goes back to an early eighteenth-century edict of Queen Anne's, which gave printers the right to run off copy (or *copyright*). It allowed publishers and printers to buy a work from an author and do what they wanted with it. For nearly three centuries, with occasional ups and downs, the tradition has flourished in northern Europe and more recently in the United States.

A contrary tradition, born in late eighteenth-century France with Beaumarchais, holds that the author of the work remains its owner, with financial and moral rights to the work. This conception, considerably developed by Victor Hugo, has gained wide acceptance. It led, at the end of the nineteenth century, to the signing of the Berne Convention, which today is subscribed to by nearly a hundred countries across the world.

This fundamental contradiction between the two traditions explains why American film, never considered an art, has for so long been the work of producers. In Europe, on the other hand (and particularly in France), the idea that film is a form of artistic expression (and even an art in its own right) has taken root and matured. Like the directors and critics who launched the New Wave, the author or authors of films, insisting on the personal nature of their work and guaranteed rights to that work by the Berne Convention, considered themselves artists on a par with painters and writers.

With this immediate consequence: if film is indeed an art, a legitimate form of cultural expression, it deserves to be given official support, even perhaps to be protected. In France this support comes from the Ministry of Culture; since 1947 it has taken different forms, chief among them a tax on cinema box-office receipts which goes to finance future film production.

The various issues that divided us during the GATT talks in no way diminish our old and lasting admiration for the enormous achievements of the American cinema. It is absurd to claim that Europe wants to shut itself off from American production, given that American images occupy seventy percent of our movie and television screens. Indeed, film seems to be part of the very flesh and blood of America. We could no more imagine America without film than we could imagine living (as the Iranians must) deprived of American film.

In fact, the whole quarrel is based on a misunderstanding. Once we have set it aside it becomes obvious that our two traditions, which have always coexisted, most often in total harmony, cannot possibly be amalgamated. It would be like asking a soccer team and an American football team to take the field together. Clearly impossible.

Nor can either tradition replace the other. They must go on coexisting. In the world ahead any kind of monopoly on the visual image would be unjust for some and dangerous for everyone.

In the discussions surrounding GATT or the North American Free Trade Agreement, the constant watchword of American negotiators was "free competition." Unfortunately, the term doesn't mean the same thing everywhere. Could we call Mali and California "free" to compete with each other? That would clearly be meaningless. The term is a nineteenth-century formulation that masks boundless economic greed. Or, as someone put it: "A free fox in a free henhouse."

What the most ferocious measures of dictatorial regimes have historically failed to achieve—the silencing of the voice of nations—a simple trading clause could still bring about. In many countries, in fact, this has already happened. In the name of "liberalizing the market" (and not always foreseeing the danger), producers and authors have lowered their guard. And the fox has come in through the front door, bringing with him basketfuls of images and sounds, but also a whole gamut of products—clothes, drinks, cereals, vehicles, cigarettes, right down to the most basic items of everyday life—all represented and often glorified by those same images.

We know too that we have embraced these moving

images as a universal language. But it is a language not every people gets to speak. Or more accurately, has the means to speak.

So at a deeper level we must ask whether the cinematographic image is necessary to nations. Is the ability to tell ourselves our own stories with the most modern means, to study ourselves in our own mirror, merely a way of enhancing life, or is it vital to life itself?

I believe it is vital to life. America's distributors say the opposite: what matter if Africans, Brazilians, even Europeans can no longer make films? We'll do it for them.

Africans are already condemned to an exclusive television diet of thrillers and romances made under alien skies, images which never speak to Africans about Africans.

The same danger threatens us.

The French production system—probably the world's most sophisticated, since it permits a mix of public and private money—represents the last square of resistance to the American invasion. If it collapses, not only French cinema will disappear, but with it the last vestiges of European cinema: farewell Wim Wenders, Andrzej Wajda, Pedro Almodóvar, Theo Angelopoulos, and so many others. And along with them every other maker of ambitious, poetic, innovative cinema (cinema still coproduced on the French model) across the world: farewell Kurosawa, Mikhailkov, Yi Mu, and Souleyman Cissé.

By defending ourselves we defend them too. Far from being "chauvinists," we are defending the right to exist of different concepts of film, wherever they may arise.

Two radically different conceptions are at war.

The two countries that invented cinema, the United States and France, once again face each other across the battle lines. What an enormous pity, particularly when you reflect that this commercial war is being waged in one direction only. No one in Europe seeks the disappearance of American film. That would be absurd and unreal. American film is and has long been massively represented on our screens, and we very much want it to stay. Ours is practically nonexistent in the USA.

The poetics of censorship.

In the early 1960s, a Czechoslovak distributor bought Vittorio de Sica's *Miracle in Milan*. He had to obtain the permission of a censorship board, but was confident in advance of success. The film was an attack on exploitation of the masses, on capitalism. He was unconcerned.

In Prague the board viewed the film. The distributor waited outside. Sternly, the chairman bore down on him and told him the film could not be shown.

The distributor was flabbergasted. Why?

The board chairman thought for a moment. Probably, like his colleagues, he had felt that the film contained unusual scenes possibly subversive of people's peace of mind (Communist regimes bought only bland, mediocre works abroad). And the end of De Sica's film actually showed swarms of homeless people flying off on broomsticks around Milan Cathedral. A cathedral, a miracle:

better not to countenance that kind of thing! But what reasons could he give? He racked his brains. Success.

"Because," he said, "anyone who knows the layout of Milan can clearly see that the homeless are flying off to the West."

Inventiveness; quick thinking. What the chairman saw in the film that day no one else had ever seen. The distributor told the story years later with undiminished resentment—but also with a certain admiration.

The dream image does not correspond to the film image. The latter is flat, enclosed within margins of clear and unchanging (or almost unchanging) configuration. It looks pinned to the wall, whereas the dream image is wobbly, imprecise, shifting, vague, like snatches of memory or hesitant ideas. A changing image, an image that eludes itself, in which the closed eye sees only its own interior, like a body flattened by centrifugal force against the damp walls of a revolving globe, in which there is no limit to the surprises and disappointments, the alarms, and sometimes the delights. The one who sees and the one seen: both together in the same bubble. Together in the same unending metamorphosis. In its best moments, the dream image of course resembles the theatre image rather than that of film.

Sometimes blindness afflicts a whole film crew. It is a collective hallucination which does not make us see but makes us not see. In a French film I worked on as both scriptwriter and actor, *L'Alliance*, directed by Christian de Challonge, not a single spectator failed to notice the splendid microphone that sat in the foreground through a whole scene. Yet no one had seen it during shooting or editing.

There are many other instances of this refusal to see. One of the most famous is the cable that held Superman aloft during one of his flights. The very first spectators saw nothing but this cable, although not a single technician had noticed it. They had to reshoot the scene in a hurry.

Another common zone in the work of actor and screenwriter: I prefer actors whose acting I do not see, in whom talent and skill have given way to a more intimate quality. I don't like to say: how well he acts! I prefer the actor to draw me closer to him, I prefer to forget he is an actor and let him transport me—as he himself has been transported—into another world.

I dislike flamboyance, overworked effects, gimmickry, intrusive makeup. The same holds for the screenplay. And of course the direction. Great art never shows its seams.

In *The Discreet Charm of the Bourgeoisie*, Michel Piccoli, who was an old friend of Buñuel's, had only one day of shooting. He played the part of a government minister.

The scene he appeared in was shot in a natural setting, a gilt-paneled drawing room. Michel Piccoli, wearing a dark suit, had just arrived, and was chatting with the crew. Buñuel drew me aside and whispered, "Just look at Michel. It's amazing. He *is* a minister!"

It was true. There was a barely perceptible change in the actor's bearing, look, and smile. Without his knowing it, an inner switch had transformed him. An impalpable metamorphosis. Where is that switch located? An eternal mystery.

Watching a film puts a particular kind of memory to work: a memory for images (settings, faces), of course, but above all "instant" memory. You have to remember a film even as you watch it. Otherwise all is lost.

Audiences have to see what they are seeing without forgetting what they have seen. At every step a whole army of faculties is wheeled into action. Some spectators are prodigiously attentive to detail. I met one young man who went to the movies only to spot errors. He found them in every film.

Special memory exercise: go in halfway through a film, see it to the end, start again at the beginning, leave. Then recall, as precisely as possible, the second half.

I recommend this highly for memory training. Perhaps also for screenwriting.

The greater the painter, the harder he makes us work. The line he proposes to us suggests rather than specifies. It challenges our eye, obliges us to finish the lines, fill in the colors. It is open; it changes as we look.

Likewise in cinema. The eye sometimes follows undrawn lines that lead it out of the frame. The eye completes the panoramic shot, finds the hidden criminal, senses the wild beast's approach, imagines the naked woman with parted legs. It is like ocean-floor charts that show rivers flowing in sharply defined beds far beneath the surface of the sea.

The same holds true for feeling, which gains from lack of precision. Great movies readily foster ambiguity and even vagueness. A look here and a gesture there will say much more about feeling than words can, or at least will say it differently. Richly drawn characters always move in an aura of uncertainty. Their behavior is not mapped out in advance, their reactions are more than mere formalities—anything can happen. As with painting, audiences will interpret in their own way what happens in bodies and on faces, different for each individual, each in his own manner absorbing and completing the character.

A permanent danger in film: simplification, reduction. Making melodrama out of tragedy. Giving black hair to traitors, fair hair to the righteous. Daily watering one's little cliché like a potted plant (the neighbors have one exactly like it).

The last scene of *Cyrano de Bergerac* takes place in autumn. The text even says so, specifying falling leaves. Knowing that the production schedule required this scene to be filmed in the month of June, director Jean-Paul Rappeneau had dead leaves stored in dozens of crates ten months in advance, ready to be strewn over the set when the time came.

He went even further. At the Spanish siege of Arras, Cyrano crosses the enemy lines every morning to mail a letter to Roxane. To afford his character better cover, and at the same time conform to historical truth, Rappeneau wanted to shoot the scene in a field of wheat as tall as wheat used to grow in the seventeenth century. He found the right seeds, well preserved, at the Museum of Natural History. In Hungary, where part of the film was shot, he had them reconstruct a seventeenth-century commonland tract, a wide field made up of several small ones. One year before shooting, this expanse was sown with tall wheat. Later, amid splendid breast-high ears, he shot not only Cyrano's breathless excursions but the great battle scene as well.

Priceless—yet unseen—work. But that particular unseen quality is the very heart of the image, without which it would not be what it is.

Another minute detail:

In Buñuel's last film, *That Obscure Object of Desire*, the wealthy Fernando Rey calls on a young Spanish girl, a poor immigrant, who lives with her mother in a dilapidated building in Paris's industrial suburbs.

The man climbs a stairway, passes somebody, and goes on to ring at a door: a very short scene, ten seconds at most.

The set for this scene was built in the studio. The day before shooting, I saw set designer Pierre Guffroy and his assistant busily scraping the walls of the stairwell, leaving barely visible marks on them. I asked Guffroy what he was up to.

He said, "The thing is, we're in a little building on the outskirts of town. The people who live here are immigrant workers, often very poor. When they can't pay their rent they sneak out, usually at night. If they can, they take their furniture along. That furniture scrapes against the walls and leaves marks. So there you are."

Signs of human habitation. Astounding research work by a great craftsman, pushing passion for logical detail to the frontiers of the imperceptible. A detail, of course, which no one would notice, but whose absence would perhaps (however vaguely) be felt.

"A challenge to common sense, a joke in loathsome taste, an offense against decency: that is the impression created by the authentically modern work," wrote Michel Leiris of Manet's *Olympia*.

What is still *modern* about the cinema?

There is something arrogant in the claim that a visual masterpiece "defies the centuries."

After a hundred years of life, film still seems fragile compared with the traditional arts. Films burn, rot, are mutilated, fade. Nothing is more complicated than seeing old films. Apparently durable stock now exists, which some claim is indestructible.

Will film then lose its first charm (inherited from the theatre), evanescence? Will it suddenly acquire the insolence of permanence?

Greater accessibility. For more than fifty years, film seemed a difficult technique, almost beyond amateur reach. Today everyone makes films, or thinks he does.

Automatic equipment for amateurs has made the professionals redundant. Uniform camera settings mean uniform images. Which means no more images at all.

Every year thousands of men and women invite their video camera along on vacation. They keep it stuck to their faces, so that they themselves see nothing, and that is how they travel. They show the world to their camera, which records it.

And they forget to travel themselves. Gone are the sketchbooks you used to see, in which hand and eye—whether skilled or amateurish—did the selecting.

Letting the camera film means not filming any more. And no one ever watches these pseudofilms, not even those who made them. For one thing, they don't have time to look at them. And it is too late now to see the world they overlooked while traveling.

Thanks to films (largely made by amateurs) showing baby grown into a young man, or dear departed grandfather, film has given a face—for the first time—to aging and death.

Cinema also exists, necessarily, outside cinemas; it is part of our daily life, part of how we dress and how we walk. Less obviously, it has also entered the paintings we look at (we readily refer to an Old Master's talent for *centering*) and the books we read. How can you avoid slipping film images between the pages of books?

An unseen film, made up of thousands of films, has infiltrated our way of looking at things. A new form dwells in us, a mobile and probably perishable form, through which we see the world. A short-lived ghost.

Forms come and go constantly. They are transmitted without the knowledge of those who use them, and often without the knowledge of those who create them.

The camera is a special eye, more different than we realize from our own. Our eye can flit from one object to the next, skipping intermediary images that are of no use to it. In a camera there is no such human way of seeing. The eye is everywhere at once; it is "inside things," as the French philosopher Gilles Deleuze said.

Everything which filmmakers put in their films but we fail to see. Everything which they fail to put in, but we do see.

When he made *El,* in Mexico, Buñuel began with the meeting of the two protagonists in a church. He made one shot of each of them as they looked at one another.

A little later in the film the two characters meet again, this time in a drawing room somewhere in town. Here again he wanted a shot of each of them, so as to stress in the most traditional style that they were predestined to meet again. Through carelessness, or because of a tight budget (he could no longer remember), he filmed only one of the two shots.

At the editing stage he was acutely aware of the absence of the second shot. Against all the rules, he decided to show in its place the same shot as in the first scene of the film. In other words, when they are actually in a social setting, one of the two characters suddenly finds himself back in the church. Everything about him is different, even his clothes.

Yet no one noticed. Buñuel even brought three or four editors together in Mexico City one day and told them: "I'm going to show you the first three reels of a film. In them is a crude mistake. Find it."

No one spotted it.

Thousands of stories of this kind are scattered through the first century of cinema. The eye's strange capacity for skating over things, seeking to see yet missing the obvious.

The opposite phenomenon also occurs. In 1992, in Poland, the filmmaker Jerzy Skolimowski undertook to direct his first play. His friends tried to convince him that the results were unpromising, that the actors were clumsily placed and performing badly, and so on. Skolimowski didn't see this at all. Then he made a video of his work and viewed it on a screen. His mistakes were immediately obvious, and he was able to rectify them. His eye had grown used to a filmed view of things. He saw nothing else.

Every form of expression we know—literature, painting, music, sculpture—has spawned by-products in swelling numbers and growing shabbiness, particularly since the nineteenth century. Film made its appearance at the busy height of the industrial era, at the very moment standardization in the manufacture of everyday objects had carried the day.

It soon fell victim in its turn. There has long been a cut-rate cinema, a bargain-basement cinema. The problem is that whatever the end result of the film, its physical appearance is everywhere the same. Format, film-stock, and presentation are similar—which makes it difficult to be selective.

Some people—François Truffaut, for instance—have called television simply a more mediocre version of cinema. I believe this is not accurate. As far as the material form goes, yes. But on television, films made for cinema are cripples, limping, mutilated in a thousand ways. Films made for television are produced faster, with less care. And when we come to the production-line TV series, the decline is obvious at once, even to the dullest eye.

But there are also good, even very good, television films. Indeed, some TV series stand comparison with the great popular novels we all love.

The opprobrium directed at television, like all opprobrium, needs tempering.

In the 1960s, certain French magazines were at a loss what to say about Buñuel. Concerned more with a director's "handwriting" than with the content of his work, they found it hard to detect any form in Buñuel's films that might be studied.

A further source of awkwardness was Buñuel's resolute determination never, never to explain the whys and wherefores of a story. Buñuel openly ridiculed certain painters, contemporaries of his, who "write more than they paint." A lofty rejection of self-explanation, which is usually either disguised self-defense or vainglorious self-justification.

Here too, the voice of the shadows.

Buñuel's films (and those of a handful of others) are beyond a doubt more than just films. Perhaps they come in the form of films only accidentally, in the absence of another, ideal form, a perfect, active form, "a form not of art."

Hence the sovereign and quite unaffected contempt Luis felt all his life for aesthetic effect, elegant framing, unusual lighting, musical accompaniment—everything that helps turn a film into an object of art. He burst into that irresistible laugh of his whenever a reporter referred to his "palette," or analyzed and classified his closeups and establishing shots.

Perhaps Buñuel's films are not films, because this so-called filmmaker was in reality a character of much broader (some would say monumental) stature. Often considered in France and elsewhere as a peripheral figure, a mere "Surrealist," he is today most solidly implanted in the culture of Spain, a granite outcrop dominating every crossroads. You can walk around him, insult him, shrug, even try to blow him to smithereens (his secret dream). But nobody can ignore him. If you are a contemporary Spanish novelist or musician, or just a man alive to the voices around you, you can do without Picasso, who is a painter and nothing but a painter. You cannot escape Buñuel. Sooner or later your paths will cross.

A character of boundless resources, he was by nature comfortable with contradictions others would have found unbearable: a nonartist creating great art; an atheist nurtured on Catholicism; an antibourgeois yet a discreetly (and charmingly) bourgeois bourgeois; and above all else a Spaniard, the very incarnation of Spain, but a banished Spaniard, who did the bulk of his work in Mexico City and Paris.

I worked with him for nineteen years, and for me he is first and foremost—beneath his open, almost innocent appearance and his liberality—the essence of secretiveness. First of all about himself. All his life he rejected psychology ("arbitrary, useless, restrictive"), refusing to explain himself, whatever the act in question, as long as that act struck him as plausible and real and allowed him to mine deep-buried treasure chambers.

I have always been struck by the two images that opened and closed his career, the first shot he ever filmed and the last. The first, still famous, from the start of *Un Chien Andalou*, shows a razor slicing the eyeball of a woman looking into the camera. The last image he filmed, at the end of *That Obscure Object of Desire*, is of a woman's hand sewing up a gash in a piece of bloodstained silk.

He set great store by that image. He even filmed it again, to improve it, two weeks after shooting was over. It was indeed his last image, as if fifty years later he somehow sought to repair that first gaping slash. Between the two—secrecy, the abyss.

Buñuel belongs more to Spain than to film historians. I know how weary he was ("bored to tears," in fact) of being likened to Goya—like him an Aragonese, like him deaf, and like him Frenchified, "adulterated" by France (*afrancesado*)—but it is impossible, even this soon, not to compare the two men. Sooner or later, wherever he may be, Buñuel will have to resign himself to it.

In 1972, George Cukor threw a big lunch in Buñuel's honor. He invited me and the producer Serge Silberman, as well as Raphael, one of Luis's sons.

An impressive guest list: John Ford, Ruben Mamoulian, William Wyler, Billy Wilder, Robert Wise, Robert Mulligan, George Stevens, Cukor himself, and Alfred Hitchcock (who sat down beside Luis, embraced him, and talked to him about *Tristana* and *Discreet Charm* throughout the meal). The two men were the same age. On a television show a few months earlier, asked which filmmakers he admired, Hitchcock had replied:

"Apart from myself, Buñuel."

Hitchcock also spoke of his cellar—his pride and joy —and its splendid wines. Alas, he could no longer drink: Buñuel sympathized most sincerely. And he ate only a small piece of boiled fish, which Cukor had had specially prepared for him.

Toward the end of lunch, toasts were proposed. Naturally there was much talk of the "good old days," of the American production system, of the stupidity of the major companies, of the thralldom of the star system. George Stevens raised his glass and said, more or less:

"Despite all that separates us, despite our different backgrounds, despite our differences of opinion, I drink to what has brought us together here."

Buñuel had the toast translated for him, raised his glass and replied:

"I drink, but I have my doubts."

* * *

Recently someone asked, "Will computers make films one day?"

He was told, "Most certainly. And other computers will go to see them."

As a child, living in the country, I saw Fritz Lang's *Metropolis*. In it I discovered my first city, and for a long time I believed that every city on earth resembled the one in the movie—full of muscular men walking with bowed heads. I also wondered whether certain flesh-and-blood women didn't conceal metallic women whose secret would be revealed only by death at the stake.

We may well spend the greater part of our life looking for the cinema monsters of our childhood. Our first monsters: unforgettable, like first loves and first thrills.

One of my finest film memories is of seeing Chaplin's *The Great Dictator*, soon after the end of the Second World War, at the Gaumont-Palace, then the biggest cinema in Paris.

It was packed. The audience was exultant. I have never known such a strong, clear sense of victory.

One of the cinema's great strengths is what might be called its capacity to animate, to give meaning and life to ordinarily inanimate objects. A famous example occurred in Renoir's *La Chienne*. In the middle of a scene

211

in a bedroom between a man and a woman, even before the idea of murder arises, Renoir inserts a closeup of a glittering letter opener lying on the bedsheets.

Abruptly, the frame introduces a third character to us. The possibility of crime has entered the picture. We have seen it. We view the scene with different eyes.

Objects have attitudes and expressions. In their own way they act and tell stories. Jean Epstein noticed this as early as 1926, in his book *The Cinematograph Viewed from Etna:*

"Once upon a time, not so long ago, there was no American drama without the revolver scene, the weapon being slowly withdrawn from a half-open drawer. I loved that revolver. It appeared as the symbol of a thousand possibilities."

Hence the care filmmakers put into choosing objects, clothing, accessories, into displaying and lighting them. A concern inherited from painting and photography, but compounded in film by the object's place in the story.

I have seen directors audition dogs and monkeys, but also shoes and bunches of roses.

Jean Epstein also said that when man appeared on film it was the first time we had seen him through an eye which was not itself also a human eye—hence the impartial "confessional" power that some attributed to the novel device.

But this is not quite true. For one thing, photography had already traveled much of the road film was to take; and besides, we all know that cameras are sentimental.

Actors endowed with what is called presence are often told, "The camera likes you."

Epstein called the cinema "a young enigma."

Roberto Matta tells how he visited Mondrian in New York one day. As he entered the studio a woman was leaving.

Mondrian greeted him and made tea. He was a taciturn, solitary, bespectacled man. To Matta—who is himself all joy and expansiveness—he seemed moody. Matta asked him why.

"It's that woman who just left," said Mondrian. "She asked me, why do you put all those straight lines in your pictures?"

When Matta said nothing, Mondrian asked him, "Well, do you see any straight lines in my pictures, Matta?"

This cautionary tale can doubtless be applied to film. What does Fellini not see in his films? Or Kurosawa? Bresson? Stanley Kubrick?

Buñuel was sincerely surprised, even sometimes irritated, when they told him *Los Olvidados* was a cruel film. He saw something quite different in it.

The storyteller's is a time-honored role. He tells men where they come from (we were all born inside a story), he weaves fables for them and adds a moral, to show them in his own way how they should behave. He amuses and teaches them. The storyteller's patron saint

is the illustrious Scheherazade, in nightly danger of losing her head if the story she conjured up failed to interest
the Sultan. Her life hung on her words. There is no
sharper symbol of the truly capital importance of the
storyteller's art.

Down through the centuries storytellers have used
myth, epic, jokes, riddles, theatre, the novel.

And finally film. The filmmaker is the heir of the
great storytellers of the past, and the keeper of their
tradition.

In film as elsewhere, the need to tell a story imposes
its own discipline. We have to follow a definite order,
include specific information, present the narrative to the
audience in coherent form. No one is forced to tell a
story, but whoever does so must be aware of the obliga-
tions ahead—not the illusion of freedom, but rigorous
discipline. Only on the basis of this discipline, bent entirely to the spectator's needs, can the author make room
for his own voice to be heard.

Which stories should we tell? The choice is up to us.
It is in fact our very first duty.

Where should we look? Where should we seek the
indispensable gift? And how should we put it to work?

Any answer has to be tentative. Some people say that
stories are born of abrupt and fleeting shifts in the course
of our lives and our feelings, of ruptures, of shocks, as if
discrete elements that had hitherto slumbered apart from
one another had suddenly been brought together.

But this is not at all certain. The notion of the shock
is certainly appealing (with its connotation of lots being
shaken up before a draw), but we also know of great

authors impervious to shock, or at least highly skilled at concealing their inner turbulence.

Much more convincing is the notion of the story-teller's kingdom as a kind of fifth or sixth dimension, in which things would have neither the same substance nor the same logic as in our own world. It would be composed of a kind of parallel matter made up of neutrinos —massless, subatomic particles permeating every one of us, but with varying degrees of force and insistence. A kingdom of ambiguity, of contradictions, but above all of limitless potential, in which thousands of characters and plots would be available in the space between nothing-ness and existence. Nor could anyone say what they were or were not. Everything would depend upon us.

This kingdom has no borders. It figures on no map. The location of the mine—deep, one hopes, inexhaust-ible, and renewable—is unknown. I remember a short story by Richard Matheson. In it, a man wonders who on earth dreams up the jokes (always anonymous, generally off-color) that do the rounds of the world's bars, news-rooms, and corporations. Obsessed by the question, he embarks on a long, arduous, dangerous search. Finally, inside a huge mountain, he finds a kind of unknown com-munications center, the mysterious source he seeks, where reporters, writers, humorists—people removed from the world and believed dead—are forced to labor in secret. The funny stories they invent are then borne all over the world by teams of talebearers. Hemingway himself, fleetingly glimpsed, is one of the unwilling workers.

The object is to hold nations and societies together

with laughter. It is an unsung but essential task. The storyteller's task.

And no one is to blame if he fails. As an old Sufi poet once said:

> *The night is over, and my story is not done,*
> *But how may I blame the night for that?*

I am struck today by the extraordinary vitality of the storytelling tradition. A vitality that comes from the remotest of pasts. It has even been attributed to cosmic forces.

Today, perhaps more than ever, we live within the stories we are told. Which explains the persistence among French filmmakers of a very hoary fear, the fear that there are no longer any good screenwriters. It is a fear that is given regular expression. But behind the ignorance that such fear betrays (our own screenwriters are neither better nor worse than others) is a genuine need, our need to hear stories. It is a permanently unrequited need. Every nation in every age has longed for better stories, for stories are the stuff of which people are made and in which they recognize and identify themselves. They want the stories they hear to be better because they themselves aspire to be better. We have never had enough screenwriters. It could not possibly be otherwise.

There are many other components to our lives. That goes without saying. We are not made up of stories alone. But without stories we are nothing, or very little.

Struck by some remarks made by the neurologist Oliver Sacks, author of *The Man Who Mistook His Wife for a Hat,* I asked him for his notion of what a "normal man" might be. Sacks hesitated, then answered that a normal man is—perhaps—one who is able to tell his own story. He knows where he came from (he has a past, a functioning memory), he knows who he is (his identity), and he thinks he knows where he is going (he has plans, and at the end of his plans lies death). He is thus situated in the flow of a narrative: he is a story.

Should this individual-story link be shattered, for whatever mental or physiological reason, that man would be ejected from time's flow. He would cease to know anything, to know who he was or what he should do. He would clutch at the appearances of existence as at a straw. From a medical standpoint he would be adrift. His bodily mechanisms would still function, but he would be lost along the way. He would no longer exist.

Can the same be said for a whole society? Many people think so. No longer to be able to tell one's story, to situate oneself satisfactorily within time, could actually trigger the disappearance of whole peoples, cut off from themselves by their memory's failure to regenerate and keep on regenerating. Cut off from themselves and perhaps driven mad.

Yet another old tale:

A man listening to stories told by a sage saw that they were interpreted sometimes in one way, sometimes in another. What was the point in telling stories, asked the man, if they were all given such different meanings?

"But that is just what gives them their worth!" answered the storyteller. "How greatly would you value a cup from which you could drink only water, but no milk? Or a plate from which you could eat only meat, but no lentils? And remember: both cup and plate are of limited capacity. What then can we say about language, which promises us an infinitely more copious, richer, and more varied diet!"

For a moment he was silent. Then he went on more gently:

"The true question is not 'What is the meaning of this story? In how many ways ought I to understand it? Can it be reduced to a single meaning?' The question is 'Can this person I am speaking to profit from what I am about to tell him?' "

THE FOG
OF I·MAGES

During the 1920s, the big Hollywood studios rebuilt the world. You no longer needed to travel, either in space or time: the planet was at your fingertips. You had only to build and to paint. Not since the vast artists' workshops of yesteryear, where camels, Roman armor, pineapples, and model galleons jostled for space around Rubens or Titian—immense but essential mountains of bric-a-brac—had so many images of this world been piled up together.

From *Intolerance* on, no challenge was too great. Crews built Gothic cathedrals, broke them up after use, erected in their place Baghdad palaces, and so on. If we could see the activity on one of those sets speeded up over a period of a few years it would give us a staggering image of our own world, chaotic, turbulent, endlessly destroyed and endlessly rebuilt.

Their inventiveness of detail sometimes bordered on the miraculous. I recall, in the original *Thief of Baghdad*, the magic carpet's *shadow* skimming over the city walls: refinement at the heart of the illusion. The cinema was an unbelievable image factory, clearly unprecedented in history. Essence of world, canned and bottled.

In the same period, privileged denizens of this microcosm—famous actors like Mary Pickford and Douglas Fairbanks—enjoyed a fabulous planetwide popularity. Their journey to Moscow in 1926 was authentic delirium. They were like heroes of legend coming from a magic land. They seemed immune to human weaknesses. When a star like Rudolph Valentino died before his time, a whole stunned world went into mourning.

Yet these films on which such meticulous care was lavished were not intended to last. Those flickering forms knew that the technical progress which had given them life also doomed them to an early old age.

A film was shot, edited, shown, forgotten.

In the same period, particularly in Europe, an eccentric notion that directly challenged this sense of impermanence came into being. The cinema, that vast carnival attraction, was an art, a new art, seventh in the line, the "art of the twentieth century." It would swiftly replace all others, usurping the functions of painting, architecture, music, literature, and of course the theatre, and finally become a "total art." No one was ever certain what "total art" might mean, but an incredible storehouse of writing on the subject is available. Some even said that the arts had been progressing and evolving since the dawn of history solely in order to arrive at the blossoming of film; past centuries, deprived of this ultimate wonder, were to be pitied.

But as we all know, reading, concerts, and the opera are nowhere near their death throes. Never have major exhibitions of painting attracted so many visitors, never has theatre seemed so vital and inventive—whereas film (particularly film considered as an art) is in crisis.

Perhaps the mistake was believing in the possibility of a kind of universal convergence, believing that the cinema could toss all known languages into the crucible of a new language, like peoples joining a federation to become just one people. The old dream of the single language, of the supremacy of one form of expression. But the cinema, a newcomer in already crowded territory, had on the contrary to find its mark of distinction (or, to use one of the buzzwords of our age, its *difference*). Its universal popularity obscured its distinctive nature, as well as its limits. It drew unheard-of crowds and created new forms of worship, but it was just another medium entering the field—and compelled, moreover, to elbow its way in.

Where does it stand today, on the verge of its hundredth birthday? I don't know. No one knows. On the one hand it still seems to be wildly self-congratulatory. No other form of human expression celebrates itself with such pomp and energy. Everywhere there are festivals, conferences, seminars, clubs, museums, award ceremonies watched by millions; they go hand in hand with prolonged waves of nostalgia (for beyond a doubt the cinema has had a golden age), as well as the whiff of smoke from its own funeral pyres.

On the other hand we have the crisis, the good old shrinking-audience crisis I have been hearing about for the past thirty years. Although it is, of course, the crisis of just one kind of film—film projected in movie houses. But all of us see more and more films, only we see them in other ways, on television, on cassette, in airplanes, in certain trains, soon perhaps in the rear seats of our cars. We are close to envisaging personalized screenings—on special goggles, on the insides of helmets: developments that will make it possible to watch a film anywhere, on the beach or in the subway, the way a Walkman permits solitary listening.

And movie houses themselves are fighting back on every front, acquiring superb projection equipment, far superior now and in the foreseeable future to present TV sets. Theatres are even adopting new processes, Omnimax, wraparound vision, sixty-frame-per-second projection. The outcome of the technical war is still very much in the balance. Audience interaction has invaded auditoriums, triggering fine brawls among spectators (it was designed to do just that). Soon, thanks to laser-scanned videodiscs, the cinema will compete with television in its own backyard, the home. Our apartments will turn into movie houses, multiscreened if we so wish; we will live inside image-walls with image-furniture and ghost-fittings made of holographic images. In a science-fiction setting of this kind (which we would be right to call nightmarish, the more so because these objects and furnishings would be literally beyond our grasp), we might invite Napoleon and Marlene Dietrich, in the form of synthetic images, to have a cup of holographic tea, listening the while to Caruso and Billie Holiday—who, if

222

we wished, could also attend in clear, convincing, and even tangible form.

We will be able (indeed, we already are able, thanks to ever-improving synthetic images) to usher real actors into nonexistent trains. With the help of outlandish equipment, still cumbersome and high-priced but bound to shed weight, we will be able to enter our computers, thus overturning all our viewpoints, our ideas, our conceptions of matter, and frolic at leisure in a mathematical garden.

There is more: we can (if we are clever enough) devise scenarios bringing together all the great performers of our youth, or even of remoter times, preserved in synthetic form. We will be able to introduce Greta Garbo to Humphrey Bogart in our homes, in settings to suit us, and—for once—have them act together. We will even be able to act along with them, speak to them, get to know them.

We can already make love with a nonexistent woman whose fragrance, skin, and intimate warmth we will feel despite her nonexistence. Within a few years we will be able to select the face, body, and voice of this woman from models offered by the agents of this new form of prostitution. Given a few ingredients, we will be able to manufacture our own models, pick Marlene's legs, Marilyn's bosom, and so forth.

We will be able to do a lot, perhaps even too much. As their name suggests, movies keep moving. Today more than ever. The cinema's path is never well marked. It has had to blaze a trail through mirage.

To be truthful, the experience of virtual reality, the appearance of new worlds at our command in whose midst we move with our thoughts and our feelings, all this poses another question: is this still cinema? What exact meaning do we even give to the word "cinema," which means different things in different languages?

Can we even think historically about "the cinema"? I doubt it. We already try much too hard, brandishing balance sheets and forecasts. Attempting to turn something into history is paralyzing if that something is one of life's currents. The cinema is everything *but* the past.

But are we beginning, despite its dazzling technical possibilities, to perceive that its powers are not so limitless as we had believed? Instead of expanding forever, could cinema's range actually be shrinking, almost without our knowledge, because of its unavoidable dependence on the physical nature of film? Has it come full circle in its hundred years? Or has the whole of this past century merely been its infancy? To reduce it to a single question: is cinema young or old?

Questions for today as for tomorrow. Impossible to answer them; otherwise they would no longer be questions.

Technical improvements are simply part of the normal course of things; they have never meant that an art form was making "progress." That word is meaningless, yet it is a trap into which we regularly fall. How often do we read or hear: "We have come a long way since the days when filmmakers couldn't . . ." or else: "Very soon the movies will finally be able to . . ."

No. We confuse things: fashion and taste, evolution and progress. Every period and every people has its own way of saying things, and the bulk of what we produce is swept into oblivion. This fate awaits us all. It is impossible to foretell "what will survive" of our time (always supposing anything at all survives). Everything, all the time, has to be started afresh. Everything, including the cinema. It is neither dead nor gloriously alive. Whatever future forms it assumes, however attractive they may seem to us, it is neither enthroned in permanent splendor nor fated for imminent demise. Like everything else, it is in motion, and in danger.

At a filmmakers' conference in Los Angeles two or three years ago, someone put the usual question to me: has "technical progress" been good for cinema? Will the medium change as a result?

I indulged myself by making up a story where someone asks Flaubert whether the replacement of the goose quill by the steel nib had changed literature. I made Flaubert (may he forgive me) reply, "I don't think so. But it has changed life for geese."

All "technical progress" has to go hand in hand with loss. In the case of the goose quill what was lost was a suppler, more personal, more animal contact with paper, not to mention the whiteness of the feather, the beguiling irregularities of its point, the application required.

The craftsman grows used to the imperfect tool. In the end he finds charm in it, in the very efforts it obliges him to make. Often we abandon it with regret, like a familiar piece of clothing whose worn fabric we found soothing. All painters have loved "accidents" of draftsmanship.

On the other hand, we willingly succumb to heady newfound facility. It blinds us to all else; we believe the problem solved (without wondering which problem). We even wonder how on earth we ever managed to live and work without this admirable discovery. And we remain virtually blind to the essential: our dearth of real invention, our miserably repetitious ideas, our very commonplace stories.

Too widespread, too trite: the image is waning. Fading into what surrounds it, what precedes it, what follows it. What is an image which we no longer see?

This eclipse of the visual is an already perceptible phenomenon. It horrifies advertisers. Nobody foresaw it. And it is the area in which our future is probably being decided.

Let us think back to the images, all of them inanimate, which a sixteenth-century householder had at his disposal: three or four prints and a few canvases on his walls; some pious faces in his book of hours; stained-glass windows in churches and public places.

In quantitative terms, very little. Qualitatively, hard to measure. "I live, but outside myself," said many of the mystic poets, who saw a very great danger in this theft of oneself, and saw as well the true kingdom in the inner image.

To what extent today are we emptied, robbed, sucked out of ourselves by the images that assail our every waking moment?

How can we escape them? How to select one or two, preserve and store them? Imbue them with new strength?

How, if you are a filmmaker today, do you create a *visible* image?

* * *

We might also wonder—we do it too rarely—about what cinema may have transformed within ourselves, how it may have changed that unseen form which dwells in each of us and which we constantly strive to adapt to the world. That form through which we see the world, through which, as the philosophers say, we somewhat fearfully *apprehend* it.

Sometimes, in fools and fanatics of all kinds, this form is fixed, congealed. Whether they are paralyzed by political or aesthetic ideologies, by religious teachings, by personal convictions, the world can bounce off them and they never turn a hair. They see it through the bars they cling to. Cinema has no hope of moving them, or at least not outwardly.

In others the form is supple and even variable, eager to adapt to the uncertainties of the real, to our illusions and contradictions. For such people—true seekers, alert travelers—the cinema's contribution is probably substantial. Its influence can extend to our external behavior, to our inner awareness, to our most hidden fantasies. At certain moments of our lives, for each of us, inevitably, cinema has given specific shape to (and has even awakened) our sexual curiosity, introduced us to the pleasures of movement, of speed, of time-travel. It has given us the disturbing itch for power, for sometimes brutal domination, for murder and war. It has exposed us to the fascination of physical strength, gleaming muscles, disproportionate, supernatural power. It has renewed our heroes and our monsters, our whores and our madonnas. In its flight its wings have brushed all our daydreams, uncovered all our hopes and vices.

Do we know ourselves better than we did before the birth of film? Clearly nobody (unless enormously arrogant) can say. We know ourselves differently. After a hundred years of moving images and sounds, our surface is no longer the same. Beneath that surface it is harder to tell. We can no more deny the existence of the cinema, both outside and inside us, than we can deny the air we breathe. It is in everyone's baggage. It has penetrated us, neglecting no area that could possibly be explored. Some filmmakers have even looked beyond everyday concerns, not just for a way of life but for a reason to live. To unite a story told in pictures with a deep questioning of life—that has been the enduring dream of the Japanese masters. Perhaps, unlike Westerners, they were unburdened by the weight of dusty centuries of metaphysical systems. Whatever the reason, the Japanese have elevated our peepshow to the place we least expected to see it, to the domain of thought, of philosophy. And the Japanese were not alone. Bergman and Fellini can also be numbered among our century's philosophers. They show us their time, which is also ours, and the mirror they hold up to us always contains some surprises about ourselves.

To what extent has the cinema changed our inner form, and in consequence our relations with the world? Are these changes hereditary? It is impossible to say. No doubt it varies from one individual to another. Even today some families forbid their children to watch television. In a way this is understandable. Thousands of hours are thus saved from passivity, from stultification, and turned to better use. But who can say what these children may have failed to acquire? What will they lack, compared to other children?

Another question: tests have apparently proved that fetuses in their mothers' wombs are sensitive to the musical signature-tunes of certain TV programs. When exposed to this soothing music in the weeks following their birth, they recognize it and are lulled to slumber. Are they not then also sensitive to the crackle of gunfire, the screech of tires, the terrified screams of women in danger? And do these very ordinary sounds from the audio-visual world, frequently heard even before they are born, warn them of the brutality of the world they must enter, like it or not, in a few weeks' time?

How film has shaped us, and daily continues to shape us, we don't really know. Beyond a doubt, though, we should ask ourselves the question and not ignore it, even if the answer is lost somewhere in the darkness within us. Like every experience of the world, film brings us back face to face with ourselves. We thought cinema was outside us, whereas it clings to us like a skin. We had assumed cinema was mere entertainment, but it is part and parcel of what we wear and how we behave, of our ideas, our desires, our terrors.

When we return to our inner theatre, we realize how destitute we are, how little we know about ourselves. In the kind of knowledge that matters, we are by definition ignorant, routinely blind. Millions and millions of images send us scrambled reflections of ourselves. Where are we? Which vision of us is the most accurate? Nothing is really certain. And we are ourselves that uncertainty.

* * *

No doubt those African dignitaries who closed their eyes to sacrilegious intrusion sensed a danger—the loss of self. The danger of being taken, of vanishing into those external images. By lowering their lids, perhaps they sought to shield themselves against that threatened loss of self.

Yet at the same time they were denying themselves a pleasure, a form of knowledge. And we face the same choice.

In a wonderful passage, Amadou Hampâté-Bâ describes how in the 1930s he urged his mother to go to the cinema and keep her eyes open. Very pious, highly reluctant, she finally complied. She sat through a French film from beginning to end, went home without speaking a word, and all night long remained shut in her room. Her son did not see her again until next day. She then told him, very calmly, after her long hours of reflection, that a people capable of creating those human forms could not have done anything wicked. On the contrary. In the old African woman's opinion, they had even risen toward the power and beauty of God.

Let us stop there, on that distant night of meditation and its radiant morning. Let that divine reference guide us through the confusion we live in. Let us be as wary of enthusiasm as of skepticism. Let us keep both a hot and a cool head. Let us never lose the desire to do or to see what others have done—but to see it properly, so that our eye extends and enlarges the screen instead of shrinking and scrambling it.

And finally, let us never forget that language, of whatever kind, is inherently deceptive. Poets have long been wary of it. The Persian Mowlânâ spoke of the "mist of speech" that shrouds true reality. To this mist of speech, the twentieth century has added the clamorous fog of images I have been trying to discuss. Fog piled, alas, upon fog! And filmed images (precisely because film looks so perfect, because it doesn't look like a mask) are perhaps the most deceptive of all the masks we set upon reality's face.

And yet, when a film takes complete hold of us, images we know to be false can lead us to a superior reality, stronger, sharper, and finally more real than reality itself.

So let us be guided by artifice and borne on illusion —just so long as we are not completely taken in. Whichever side of the image we happen to be on—whether as filmmakers or filmviewers—we have in common this fog which enfolds and inhabits us. From time to time it lifts and is pierced by shafts of light. Then it rolls in again.

And yet, whether light or fog, the filmed image so far constitutes the only victory we have ever won over death. Film is a continuation of life, with the appearance of life prevailing over the appearance of death. We live forever with our ghosts.

The physical quality of these ghosts constantly improves. One day perhaps they will sit down to table with us, get into bed with us. One day we will marry ghosts.

And the fact that ghosts notoriously cling to their places of origin (hoary Highland castles, for example) gives us one more good reason for continuing to manufacture our own.

No doubt that was what the old Africans feared: invasion by alien (and perhaps living) forms, bent on taking possession of them. Necessarily dangerous ghosts in which (unlike Hampâté-Bâ's mother after her sleepless night) they fail to recognize the marks of a new creation.

ABOUT THE AUTHOR

Jean-Claude Carrière is the president of FEMIS, France's only film school. He has written screenplays for more than fifty films, including *The Discreet Charm of the Bourgeoisie, The Tin Drum, The Unbearable Lightness of Being, The Return of Martin Guerre,* and *Cyrano de Bergerac,* a dozen plays, and many books.